On the Edge of Nowhere

On the Edge

of

Nowhere

by James Huntington as told to Lawrence Elliott

Foreword by Gregory Frank Cook

Epicenter Press Inc.
Alaska Book Adventures™

Epicenter Press is a regional press publishing nonfiction books about the arts, history, environment, and diverse cultures and lifestyles of Alaska and the Pacific Northwest.
For more information, visit www.EpicenterPress.com.

Text copyright ©2002 Jimmy Huntington Foundation and Lawrence Elliott. Cover photographs copyright ©2002 Alaska Stock Images. Third Edition published by Epicenter Press, 2002 Second Edition published by Press North America, 1991 First Edition published by Crown Publishers, 1966

Photographs by Lawrence Elliott

All rights reserved. No part of this publication may be reproduced, stored in a retrieval system, or transmitted in any form by any means, electronic, mechanical, photocopying, recording, orotherwise, without the prior written permission of the publisher. Permission is given for brief excerpts to be published with book reviews in newspapers, magazines, newsletters, catalogs, and online publications.

ISBN: 978-1-935347-29-3 (eBook)
ISBN: 978-1-941890-49-3 (Print)

Library of Congress Control Number 2002111725

10 9 8   11 12 13 14 15 16 17 18 19 20

Table of Contents

Forward

    Gregory Frank Cook

Chapter One   1

    My Mother

Chapter Two   25

    My Father

Chapter Three   49

    Growing Up

Chapter Four   77

    Living on the Land

Chapter Five   121

    Dogsled Racing

Chapter Six   165

    Starting Over

Afterword   175

FOREWORD

Jimmy Huntington used to say, "Where there's life there's hope."

It was his maxim for survival in the wilderness, as when he fell through the ice on a sub-zero day and had about five minutes to get a fire going with wet wood and numb fingers before he froze to death. It was also his philosophy of life, and he said it so often that it became a joke between us, as when he pointed out a pretty girl across the street with an old man's shaking hand and we both spoke together: "Where there's life there's hope."

We met when Jimmy was on the Fisheries Board, the toughest job in Alaska, and I was executive director. It fell on the shoulders of the seven Board members to make the regulations for the conservation and management of all the fisheries resources in this immense state—commercial fishing, a multi-million dollar industry; subsistence fishing, the life blood of the Native villages; sport fishing, a pillar of tourism, Alaska's third biggest moneymaker—and that was the easy part. To cut up this pie, to decide who gets what, to take a stand in the fierce competition between this region and that, between seiners, gill netters, trollers, crabbers—that was the hard part.

The Board met between 50 and 80 exhausting 12-hour days a year, taking public and scientific testimony all over the state, deliberating and voting. Almost without exception, Jimmy came down on the side of the little guy. And at the end of each day, he and I, sharing a room in some hotel or boarding house, would walk home in the cold night rehashing the testimony and the decisions and, if we were lucky, find a place where Jimmy could "warm up" with a banana split.

Somewhere along the line, he "adopted" me, although I wasn't sure I deserved it. But along with the honor came invitations to go hunting and trapping with him, and let me tell you, that beat the daylights out of Alaska Fisheries Board meetings.

At that time—it was in the early 1980s—Jimmy lived in a small log cabin downriver from the village of Huslia on the south bank of the Koyukuk. It was decorated to his taste: on the wall hung a fan made from the tail feathers of a spruce grouse, and a white ermine skin; a faded panel of wood nailed up near the door said, "Carnation Milk From Contented Cows." The landscaping consisted of a stand of short spruce and birch trees typical of the latitude. But they were tall enough to hide a bear so you never went far from the cabin without a rifle.

One September I came flying up to Huslia to join Jimmy on a moose hunting trip, excited as a kid with his first rifle. We traveled in Jim's river boat, running for days on end through the endless untouched forests of interior Alaska. My most cherished memories of those crisp cold days along the Koyukuk and Yukon are of Jimmy calling over his shoulder, "Grab the grub box—time for tea." We would beach the boat and I would gather wood while Jim "made fire" and roasted moose ribs, and we ate and talked and enjoyed the feeble heat of the midday sun less than 50 miles south of the Arctic Circle. One night a foolish black bear tried to rob our cache of moose meat and wound up hanging on the drying rack beside the moose.

Another year we spent a month trapping beaver at the base of the south slope of the Brooks Range. We were in the woods through all of a bitterly cold February, sharing a small canvas tent, sleeping on top of spruce boughs and using birch bark to start the morning fire. In my mind's eye I still see the Jimmy Huntington of that magic time, moving ahead on his snowshoes, ax in hand, utterly at home in the wilderness, happy as a man can be.

Anyone who knows me knows that my teenage daughter Slim is the light of my life. And one of my devout wishes for her is that sometime in her life she comes to know as solid and singular a human being as Jimmy Huntington.

—Gregory Frank Cook

CHAPTER ONE

My Mother

MY MOTHER WAS ATHABASCAN, born around 1875 in a little village at the mouth of the Hogatza River, a long day's walk north of the Arctic Circle. The country was wild enough—blizzards and sixty-below cold all the winter months, and floods when the ice tore loose in spring, swamping the tundra with spongy muskegs so that a man might travel down the rivers, but could never make a summer portage of more than a mile or so between them.

And the people matched the land. From the earliest time in Alaska, there had been bad feeling between Indian and Eskimo, and here the two lived close together, forever stirring each other to anger and violence. If an Indian lost his bearings and tracked the caribou past the divide that separated the two hunting grounds, his people would soon be preparing a potlatch to his memory, for he was almost sure to be shot or ground-sluiced, and his broken body left for the buzzards. Naturally this worked both ways. Then, in the 1890s, prospectors found gold to the west, on the Seward Peninsula, and the white man came tearing through. Mostly he was mean as a wounded grizzly. He never thought twice about cheating or stealing from the Native people, or even killing a whole family if he needed their dog team—anything to get to Nome and the gold on those beaches.

And once, through two winters and a summer, my mother, who looked like a child and weighed less than ninety pounds, walked a thousand miles across this desperate land to get back to her home and her two children.

Her name was Anna, and her father was a Native trader. All year he traded among his own people. Then, with the first long days of March, he would make his way down the Hogatza to the head of the Dakili River, the divide between the Eskimo and the Indian lands, and there he would meet Schilikuk, the Eskimo trader. This was permitted because each needed things that only the other had, and it was the only known peaceful contact between the two races.

As soon as Anna was old enough, she began to accompany her father on these trips, and so she learned the Eskimo language. They would load up the sled with their goods and set off toward the Dakili, a five-day trek for a good strong dog team, and make camp on the south slope of the boundary hills. This was as far as it was safe to go. On the other side, Schilikuk the Eskimo would be making his way south along the Selawik River, and the great trading ritual was about to begin. In all the years that Anna went with her father, it never changed.

First the old man would walk, alone and unarmed, to the top of the divide. He carried only a long pole. If he saw no sign of the Eskimo trader he would stick his pole straight up in the snow and return to camp. Every day that it was not storming he walked back up the long hill, looking to see if a second pole had been stuck in the snow alongside his. That was the sign that Schilikuk had arrived, and that trading would begin the next good day.

Then my mother would help pull the sled up the hill—they could not use the dogs for the two teams would have fought to the death—and they would lay everything out on the snow. There were tanned hides, and wolverine fur for parka ruffs. There was a mound of soft red rock found only along the Koyukuk, which could be dipped in water and used to paint snowshoes a brilliant red. Meanwhile the Eskimo was laying out his stuff, too—salt from the Bering Sea and seal skins to make mukluks, a kind of boot worn in the spring and fall to keep out the wet.

Making believe they couldn't care less, the two traders would then inspect each other's goods. Say the Eskimo wanted a handful of red rock. He would pick it up, walk over to his own pile of things and toss a seal skin off to the side. That meant he was offering to pay that much for the rock. If my grandfather wasn't satisfied—and of course it was part of the ritual that he had to pretend to be insulted by the first offer—he would pull a second skin out of the Eskimo's pile. This was Schilikuk's signal to look hurt. He'd snatch back both skins and they'd have to start all over again.

All this took a long time and a lot of patience. There

was always the danger of tempers really flaring, and day after day there was the hard work of hauling the sled back up to the top of the divide. Once Anna told her father: "You could trade everything on the first day if you didn't have to go through that business of acting mad at each other."

My grandfather smiled: "Ah, but the Eskimo's sled is heavier than mine. Soon he will get tired of pulling it up the hill and then I will be able to buy his goods cheaply."

Years later Schilikuk the Eskimo would tell my mother that he had used exactly the same strategy.

In 1901 my mother was married to a trapper named Victor Biffelt, and they built their cabin close to the place where the Hogatza runs into the Koyukuk. They had two children, Fred and Edith, and were happy together, although the country was very lonely. They were five days' journey from Anna's people, and the only neighbor was a white man, a hothead called Ned Regan, four miles downriver. And with all that great land to trap in, Regan and Biffelt got into an argument over a certain trap line.

"Clear that line or I will kill you," Regan warned, which was the wrong thing to say to Biffelt. He had lived off the land all his life and felt he could take care of himself. Though he might have listened to reason, he was not about to be run off by threats.

"Try it," he said, "and you are the one who will wind up dead."

After that he watched the land for signs of the white man and always kept his rifle within quick reach. But even the most cautious man is liable to drop his guard in his own cabin, and that was the chance Regan waited for. One winter afternoon, with the last daylight fading in the woods, Biffelt was sitting at his table over a cup of tea. My mother was feeding her babies. With no warning, the door was flung open and there stood Regan, a shotgun at his shoulder. "Die," he said, "and be damned to you!" He pulled the trigger and, at a distance of eight feet, shot Biffelt full in the face. Then he backed out of the doorway and calmly walked off.

My mother, still holding one of the babies, could not believe what her eyes saw. Her husband, who never even had a chance to go for his gun, was a horrible sight as he sprawled dead in the chair. In the barest second her whole world had been torn apart and she was stunned with grief and shock. Years later she remembered how hot tea ran off the table from the overturned cup.

At last she realized that the children were crying and that she had to do something. She eased Biffelt to the floor and covered him with a blanket. But when she went to close the door and saw the tracks of Regan's snowshoes disappearing toward the woods, she knew that she could not stay in the cabin that night. She was suddenly afraid of many things, but mostly that the white man would come back to kill her and the two children. She must take them away, and she must leave at once.

She gathered some food and put the children in the sled. She wrapped blankets and skins around them, and with the dragline around her shoulders began hauling them up the frozen Hogatza toward its mouth a hundred miles away, where her people were. Soon it was so dark that she had to guide herself by the looming bank, but she pulled on. Not for four hours did she stop, and even then she sat up wide-eyed and watchful through most of the night, listening for the crunch of a snowshoe downriver.

"I had my man's gun," she said. "If the other one came, I would have shot him."

For five days she pulled the sled northward, always looking back over her shoulder and alert for any sign of trappers from her village. But there were none, and when she finally reached her father's house, she shook with exhaustion and hunger. When she told him of the murder of her husband, the old man looked off into the distance, and anger and sadness were on his face.

"It would satisfy me to kill him myself," he finally said. "But the white man's law says that we may no longer kill our enemies. Let us see, then, how they will deal with one of their own."

He sent his oldest son, Hog River Johnny, overland to the trading post of Ed Monson on the Kanuti River. Monson was one white man who had been fair to the Native people, and my grandfather hoped he would do the right thing. He did. When Johnny told him what had happened, he wrote a letter to the marshal at Nome, the only law officer in western Alaska, and sent it out to Fort Gibbon on the Yukon with two Indians. It finally reached the marshal just before breakup, and in April he ordered a deputy to take a dog team out and find Regan.

Although Alaska is a big land, it is a hard one to hide in. People are scarce, and so they are noticeable. By asking in the Native villages along the Yukon, the deputy soon picked up Regan's trail. He had apparently left the Hogatza and was making his way downriver. In June, the lawman caught up with him a few miles from Nulato and placed him under arrest. Then he started back to Nome with the prisoner, stopping at Koyukuk to send word that Biffelt be properly buried. But the body had lain in that cabin for five months, and the animals had broken in and there was not much left to bury.

After a time the court sent two men to fetch my mother to Nome so she could be a witness at Regan's trial. She didn't want to go—Nome was in Eskimo country, a thousand miles to the west, and she would have to be separated from her babies all winter—but my grandfather said that unless she told what had happened, Regan would go unpunished. Anna and the two deputies went by riverboat down the Koyukuk and Yukon to St. Michael's, then crossed Norton Sound to Nome on the last steamboat of the summer, arriving early in September, 1904.

It was a bewildering place for a Native girl. She had never seen so many thousands of people, nor felt so completely lost as she did in their bustle and confusion. Since she could not stay with the Eskimos, the court paid a white couple to shelter her until the trial began, and though they treated her well, every day was an agony of loneliness and homesickness. She was afraid to walk in the streets of the city, and so through each long day she sat in her little room and thought about her children and wept. Sometimes she went alone to the beach and looked out over the frozen sea and tried to imagine what it would be like when the ice finally broke up in summer and the steamboat came and she could go back home.

The trial was held in February, 1905, and of course Anna was the only witness. Regan denied that he had killed anyone. When it was my mother's turn to testify, she was afraid and spoke poorly—she knew only a little English—and they could not find anyone to translate her Athabaskan dialect.

Whether it was because of this, or because a jury of white men could not bring themselves to take the word of a Native against one of their own, Regan was found not guilty and freed of all charges.

When this was explained to my mother, she was heartsick. She tried to tell them what an awful mistake they were making, but they shrugged and said there was no more they could do. Slowly and alone she walked back to the house where she was staying and made a light pack of her few possessions.

"What are you doing?" the woman of the house asked her.

"I am going home," Anna said.

The woman, a kindly person, tried to talk her out of it. She said that no one could hope to walk such a distance across northern Alaska in the dead of winter. "Wait until breakup," she said. "Stay here with us until the steamboat comes. Then the court will send you back."

"I want nothing from the court. They took me from my children and made me stay the winter in this place. And for what? They have freed the man who murdered my husband, and now he is better off than I am."

When the woman realized that she could not stop my mother from leaving, she gave her some food and a note. "I have written down what you are trying to do," she told her. "Show this paper to anyone you meet on the trail and they will help you." Then they walked together to the edge of the town and, at the last minute, the woman put two gold coins in Anna's hand. "Good-bye," she said. "May God walk with you."

And my mother started off on her long journey home.

She was bound north, across the Seward Peninsula toward the village of Candle. All she knew of the land was that somewhere beyond Candle, a three days' walk, some said, was the place where the Kobuk River emptied into the salt water. She remembered that Schilikuk, the Eskimo trader, lived somewhere along the Kobuk, and she reasoned that once she found its outlet she could follow it east into the hills dividing Eskimo and Indian territory. From there she would know the way to her father's village.

In the beginning the trail north was not hard to follow. It had been pounded into the snow by many men headed for the placer mines around Candle. After a few days, though, it forked many times, and each time Anna had to wait for hours—once for two days—until some prospector came along and pointed her in the right direction. She traveled from sunup until dark, wrapping herself in a blanket and burrowing into a snowbank by a small fire at night. Sometimes she caught a rabbit in a snare trap, and there were three roadhouses along the way where she stopped for food and rest. In each one she offered her gold coins in payment, but the owners would read her note and refuse to take any money. Word spread up and down the trail about "the little squaw with the pack on her back," and men tried to warn her that she was trying to do an impossible thing. But they soon saw that she was bound to push on, and all they could do was wish her luck.

She reached Candle in the last days of March, her boots worn to shreds and her body shriveled with cold and hunger and a terrible weariness. A miner, who had heard of her coming, sent his wife to take her into their house. There she stayed for many days, making a new pair of boots and regaining her strength, for the worst part of the journey was still ahead. And one morning in late April, she thanked her friends for their goodness and set out again.

Now there was no more trail to follow. Each fair morning Anna put her right shoulder to the sun and pushed out across the snow-covered land. In this way she could travel ten, sometimes twelve miles before dark. But there were days when the sun didn't shine, and others when blinding gray storms trapped her where she was, holed up in a snow shelter in the midst of an endless emptiness, so that weeks passed and she had not yet found the Kobuk River. Still she pushed on.

One morning a rifle shot shattered the great stillness around her, then another. Anna looked up and saw a ptarmigan fall from the flock wheeling across the eastern sky. She shouted and stumbled across the snow, past caring about the danger that the unseen hunter might be an Eskimo. Soon she saw him, a grizzled old white man by a sled, a prospector who stood gaping at the sudden appearance of this childlike figure on the bare land. Anna fumbled loose her note and gave it to him, and when the old man had read it he shook his head in greater astonishment yet. "You can't possibly make it," he told her. "The river breaks up soon and that whole country'll flood out. Better climb on the sled and let me haul you back to Candle."

My mother thanked him but said that she had to go on. "Where is the Kobuk River?" she asked.

He pointed to the Northwest. "Another two days, maybe three. But that's only the beginning, sister. Once that ice breaks. . ."

Then he looked at Anna's face and stopped, for he saw, as the others had, that there was no use arguing with her. He gave her the ptarmigan and some matches and wished her well. He was the last human she was to see for a hundred days.

On the third morning, as the old man had said, she came to the Kobuk and turned east, following its frozen, twisting path up into the reaches of the Waring Mountains. With each passing day the sun rose higher in the big sky and the hours of daylight grew longer. Slowly the white land began to thaw, showing itself in widening brown patches on the slopes. In her father's village, Anna knew, this would be a time of gladness and expectancy. The summer was coming, and soon the Hogatza would run red with fat salmon fighting their way upstream to spawn, and the great caribou herds would sweep across the tundra, and there would be as much fish and meat as anyone wanted to eat.

For her, though, it was a time of toil and brewing danger. She sank into the melting snow with each step and the icy hummocks sucked at her boots, and every foot forward was a struggling preparation for the next. When the moon shone she traveled by night, for the land froze again soon after each sundown. By day she listened uneasily to the groaning of the Kobuk, the thawing ice cracking and grinding as it thrashed to break free.

It went out with a great unexpected thundering on a warm May morning, the sudden surge of choked water thrusting great islands of ice fifty feet in the air, and flinging lesser pieces out on both banks. Terrified, Anna staggered away over the swampy land toward a piece of high ground to the south, crawling when she fell, and reaching safety only moments before the riverbanks exploded in coils of water that had finally broken through the winter-long dam of ice. For days she sat on her barren little island, cut off by the swirling flood, unable even to build a fire for want of wood. Finally the waters ebbed. Carefully she picked her way over the drowned land to the river. And sometimes following a sandy beach beneath the bank, sometimes hauling her way through the clutching tundra, she began moving east again, down from the mountains.

She had long since eaten all the food in her pack. She had no more luck snaring rabbits, but now and then found the uneaten parts of one, or of a ptarmigan, that a marauding hawk had dropped, and she ate those. She picked berries, many of them not yet ripe, and afterward lay writhing for hours until the great pain in her stomach went away. Mosquitoes sprang up from the bog and swarmed at her face. She made a fire only on the coldest nights, for her supply of matches was nearly spent.

One day when it was well into July and she was lightheaded with hunger, she came to a hill that seemed, somehow, to have a familiar look. Hope flared and gave her strength, and she went stumbling to the top, her mind's eye already seeing the well-remembered lay of land that sloped down into Indian country. But when she looked out across the tundra it stretched away to a far horizon as strange as every one she had struggled up to in all the weeks past. She was lost in this bleak and forbidding land, still a terribly long way from home, and weary of fighting mosquitoes and the endless miles.

Suddenly sick at heart as well as in body, she let her weight carry her shakily back down to the river. She was very weak now and when she fell to her knees, she hadn't the strength to get up. She dragged herself to the bank and dug up some roots and ate them. Then she lay back in the hot sun unable any longer to fend off the mosquitoes, and listened to the hushing flow of the Kobuk, and fell asleep.

It was still daylight when she woke. She had a sharp sense of some sudden danger and half-rose as she searched the bank for a bear. Then she turned toward the river.

Watching her from his kayak, not twenty feet away, was a young Eskimo boy. For a tense and endless moment they stared at each other. And the instant Anna moved to scramble up the bank in flight, the boy's paddle flashed and the kayak shot upstream and vanished at the first bend.

Anna slumped to the ground again. She knew what must happen now—the boy would return to his village and a war council would be called and they would dispatch a party of hunters to find her and kill her—but she simply hadn't the strength to get up and run away. She made up her mind to stay where she was for one full day. Maybe when she had rested she would be able to strike out across the tundra, hiding there, away from the river, until the Eskimos came and went and the danger was past. If the boy had as much as a day's journey up the river to his village, she would have a chance. Exhausted, she pulled the blanket over her head to keep off the mosquitoes, and tried to sleep.

In the night she heard forbidding sounds, sometimes an animal growl, sometimes voices that sounded like her mother and father warning her to be careful, and she tore loose from these nightmares weaker than ever. Not long after sunrise, though, she dragged herself erect and started out over the empty land. She moved very slowly, resting with every few steps, and hadn't gone two hundred yards when the Eskimos came.

They saw her first, as soon as they came paddling around the river bend. She was up on the tundra, her bent figure plain against the open sky as she moved unsteadily among the hummocks. They hailed her and saw her stop, her shoulders sagging in defeat.

Anna stood without turning. She had tried very hard to return to her children. She had done her best. But she knew now that, alone, she could not hope to win out over the pitiless arctic. Even if the Eskimos had not found her, she was too spent with hunger and fatigue to go on any longer. Listening to them sloshing toward her across the tundra, she waited without fear, but with a great sadness, for the end.

Close behind her, one of them spoke: "Do not be afraid, my child. We have come to help you."

Anna turned around. She saw that the man who spoke was Schilikuk, the Eskimo trader, the friend of her father. With him was the young boy she had seen on the river yesterday. Tears came to my mother's eyes and she could not say anything, but the old man understood. He gave her pack to the boy and held her, and he said, "I saw your father not two moons ago. He had had word that you left Nome on foot. He asked me to watch for you. Each day my son has come down the river to wait. And now you are safe."

They helped her back to the bank and built a fire. They warmed broth and fed it to her, then the meat of a roasted duck. When she could eat no more, they put her on some caribou skins in the bottom of the boat and began paddling upstream. For the first time since she had left Candle so long ago, Anna slept with a satisfied stomach, and without fear.

When they reached the old man's village, his wife and daughter and an older son were waiting by the river. The women helped Anna out of the boat and put her to bed. Then the old man called the people to his house and said, "This woman is the daughter of the Indian trader, the one who supplies us with hides and red rock. He is my friend and no harm shall come to his child while she is under my roof. Is it understood?"

The people nodded and went away. And watching, Anna wondered how the great fear between Indian and Eskimo had begun, for these she had seen seemed no different from her own people.

The old man sat on the floor by her bed. "You will stay here with us until it is time to trade again in the spring," he said. "Then I will take you to your father."

But Anna shook her head. "I cannot wait so long," she told him. "I have been separated from my babies for almost a year and I am sick to see them."

The old man thought for a moment. "Then you must stay at least until the snow falls," he said. "By that time you will be strong again and able to travel, and the walking will be better."

Anna touched his hand in thanks. Soon she fell asleep again.

Before long she was well enough to help with the cooking and take her turn walking down to the river to empty the fish wheel. Little by little she grew close to the daughter, who was almost her age. Together they would pick berries, smoke and hang the salmon, and walk along the riverbank telling each other of their lives. Often, when Anna spoke of her dead husband, or of her children and her mother and father, she would be overcome with loneliness and sorrow. Then the daughter would hold her hand and comfort her. "The days are flying by," she would say. "Soon you will be with your loved ones again."

Fall came early that year. In September, ice was already moving in the river. Anna passed long hours searching the sky for the first hint of snow. "When will it come?" she asked the old man.

And he smiled and told her, "In its own good time,

child. A hungry fisherman may watch the river day and night, and still there will be no salmon until they are ready to spawn."

Then one morning she woke to a strange new stillness on the land. She sprang from the bed and ran to look out. During the night a steady snow had fallen and now the tundra was overlain with a soft white sheath many inches thick.

"It snowed!" Anna cried out, clapping her hands with excitement and rousing all the family. "Oh, it snowed, and now I can go home!"

They came to stand beside her, and the old man put a hand on her shoulder. "We are happy for you," he said, "though our family will be lessened when you go."

"May I leave today?"

"No, no. It is a long way and we must make preparations."

Soon the family was to leave for the head of the Pah River where they would spend the winter trapping, the old man explained. Anna would go with them, and from there would have only a ten-day walk across the divide and down to the Hogatza. First, though, the sons must go off to hunt. When they returned with meat for the trip, the river would be frozen solid and they would be ready to start.

The next days passed very slowly for my mother. The family busied themselves preparing for the journey—the sons off stalking the caribou, the old man making the snowshoes Anna would need for covering the flat timber country on the far side of the divide, and the women packing supplies onto the sled. Anna did what she could to help, but her heart was already far up the river, and she could almost see the familiar hills that were her gateway to home.

Then at last the sons returned with plenty of meat, and enough new snow had fallen so the heavily loaded sled rode easily, and the old man said they would leave with first light. That night, the chief and village council ordered a great feast for Anna, and all the people turned out, for they had come to regard her as one of their own. Food was piled high on the willow floor of the Kashim, a sort of community hall—caribou flanks and muktuk, which is the raw meat of a whale's flipper and considered a great delicacy by the Eskimos, and dried fish and a sort of ice cream made with fish meal, seal oil, and low bush cranberries—and the drummers played while the people sang and danced far into the night. At the end, each one came to my mother and took her hand, not saying anything, but bidding her good-bye in their own silent way.

Just after dawn, they closed up the cabin and made their way down to the river. The sons hooked the dogs into their traces and, with the older one walking ahead to break trail, they moved off in a single file, their breath hanging on the still, frozen air. By midmorning snow began to fall and the going grew heavy. No one could ride, for the sled was fully loaded, and they stopped frequently to rest. Still, they had covered twenty miles by dark, and the old man was well satisfied. He calculated that they had little over a hundred miles more to go.

Each day was much like the last, the silent miles of plodding through the snow, the bright campfire at night, and the dreamless sleep that follows great exertion. Then they would be off again. The long hours of hauling the sled made the dogs ravenously hungry. They wolfed down their food and yowled for more, and soon the meat supply had shrunk to practically nothing. Twice they stayed over an extra day while the sons struck out into the woods to hunt, and it was November before they reached the family's wintering place on the Pah River. And the morning after they had made their permanent camp, the old man said to Anna, "Come, I will walk with you to the divide and see you safely into Indian country."

The good-byes were sad. They all knew how unlikely it was that they would ever see one another again. The daughter, losing her friend, cried, and the old mother put Anna's hand to her mouth and held her tight until Schilikuk grew impatient. "Good-bye," Anna said. "Good-bye, my good friends."

Her eyes were filled as she followed the old man out across the sea of untouched snow, but she kept them raised to the distant hills. In three hours time they reached the top of the divide, and the Eskimo stood searching the wooded land below. Then he said, "This is as far as I dare take you, child. I can do no more." He gave her meat and dried fish, and pointed in the direction of the Hogatza. "If you lose your way, come back to these hills. We will be on the Pah until the days are long again, and will care for you until I can take you to your father."

They looked a long time into each other's eyes, then the old man said, "Go now, child," and Anna started off down the hill. Once again she was alone on the cold and empty land.

All day she walked, and came to the Hogatza just before dark. She made a fire beneath the heavy spruces and ate some meat, but could not fall asleep for many hours. For now, with all the long months and the bad things behind her, her children and her people seemed very near.

Had they given her up for dead? Would the babies even know who she was?

Next day, she quickly realized that she was not so close to her family after all. Along all the length of the Hogatza that she could see to the south, the land looked as strange and unfriendly as ever, for she had never been here in winter. But she knew now that if she had to crawl the rest of the way on hands and knees, she would get back to her Native village.

By the tenth day her food supply was very low. She wasted the morning trying to snare a rabbit, then decided to move on and try again at her next camp. She had not gone far when she came upon snowshoe tracks leading away from the river. A great dizzying joy took hold of her —they must have been made by one of her people!—and without thinking she began following the tracks out across the open snow. Not until the darkness fell did she suddenly realize what a great risk she had taken. As long as she followed the river, she knew where she was going, and could always make her way back to her Eskimo friends. Here, though, out on the open tundra, she was at the mercy of those tracks. If the wind blew them smooth in the night, or they were buried under a fresh snowfall, she would be lost on this vast and unknown white plain, without a landmark to guide her forward or back.

The night was long and seemed full of bad omens, a rushing wind and, one by one, the stars flickering out, and then the moon, as thick clouds slid under the sky. In the first gray daylight she searched for the tracks, found them, and pushed on, not even pausing for a morning meal. At midday, she noticed in the distance that the land seemed to fall away, and she hurried on, a certain unaccountable eagerness touching her heart. By the time she reached the last of the high ground she was pushing her snowshoes forward as hard as she could, and then she stood looking down, remembering, understanding the great pounding happiness that had hold of her. She knew where she was. Just below her lay the Hogatza River again, and the tracks she had followed had saved her many miles, cutting overland at the narrow neck of the river's last wandering loop before it ran into the lakes that fed its mouth. She was perhaps three days walk from her father's village. And his winter cabin was on the far bank, not five miles upriver. Would he be there? Would she be safe in his arms before this very day passed?

Full of new drive, Anna took off her snowshoes and clambered down the bank. Now she no longer needed to follow the tracks. Every twist and turn of the river was hauntingly familiar. Here she had snared rabbits from the time she was a girl—even now a snare line was strung there!—and there she used to slide down the shallow bank on the sled her father made her. With every step her spirits soared and her heart raced, and when she saw a thin line of smoke climbing into the sky ahead, tears of joy came to her eyes and she gave thanks, for she knew her father was only a shout away.

She wanted to call out to him at once, to run to him with all the last of her strength. Instead, she forced herself to sit in the lee of the bank and eat whatever scraps of food were left in her pack, for she did not mean to totter into her father's cabin hungry and exhausted. She would walk up to him straight and strong, and proud.

Soon she was ready. Holding herself in check, she moved slowly to where the tracks led up the bank, and in the last light saw the cabin, exactly as it had always been, set solidly among the alders, a place of safety and warmth. But as she took a step toward it, the dogs suddenly sensed her presence and came alive with a fierce and fearful howling. Almost at once the cabin door was thrown back and a man came bolting out, rifle up and eyes peering through the dimness for the first sign of an enemy.

"It is me," Anna called into the clamor of the barking dogs, the Indian language strange on her tongue after all these months. "I have come home."

The shadowed figure by the cabin tried to quiet the dogs. "Who is it?" he shouted. "Who's out there?"

"It's Anna. I have come home."

She saw the man's gun fall as he started toward her. "Anna," he said softly. "My sister. My little sister!"

Then he was running, and they came together with a great cry of joy, and clung to each other, Anna and her brother Johnny. They did not speak for a long time, but only held each other and looked at each other. At last Anna asked if her children were well, and Johnny told her they were. He led her to the cabin where Mary, his wife, kissed her in gladness and gave her hot tea from the stove.

"It has been such a long time," Johnny said, "a year and two moons. No one—almost no one—believed that you could still be alive. Everyone said you would be lost in that strange land, or killed by the Eskimos. Only our mother kept saying that you would return. She sent us here to stay the winter, to wait. She said that you would come walking up the river one day, and that there must be someone here to meet you."

"And our father? Does he believe I am dead, too?"

Her brother looked away. Anna, weak with happiness and relief, was suddenly cold with fear. "What is it?" she whispered. "What has happened to my father?"

"He sickened with the fever late in summer," Johnny said, still not looking at her. "He was dead before the first frost."

Anna felt her open hand go to her mouth, and knew she was holding it there to keep from sobbing aloud. She wanted to tell her brother how terribly unfair it was, but could not speak. So she sat crying, and thinking that now her father could never know that she had survived, nor how his Eskimo friend had saved her. There were so many things she had meant to tell him.

"Until the very last he asked for you," Johnny was saying. "And when he knew that he had to die, he told us not to be sad because now he would be able to watch over you from heaven."

And perhaps he had, Anna suddenly thought. Perhaps he knew she was alive, after all. And in a little while she dried her eyes and began to eat the food Johnny's wife brought her.

They talked far into the night. Anna told of her trip, and Johnny told of all that had happened to their family since she went away. It was decided that he would leave for home early in the morning, for walking alone he could bring the good news to their mother in three days. Anna was to rest one full day, then she and Mary would load all the winter supplies on the sled and follow with the dog team.

But Johnny must have run most of the way. The women had not been on the trail three days when two teams came bounding downriver to meet them. Anna was put on an empty sled and the driver drove those dogs as though chased by a bull moose, reaching the village just before nightfall.

Though news of Anna's return had spread like wildfire, the people who stood watching as the team came mushing up from the bank stared at her as they would at a ghost. No hunter, let alone a frail girl, had ever crossed the great reaches of that strange land to the north. To these people, Nome was in another world, and all the thousand miles in between a blizzard-ridden unknown, full of devilish Eskimos and constant danger. That Anna had walked it, alone and unarmed, was to them a miracle.

When she got off the sled, they fell back to make a path for her. A few called out a welcome, but Anna could not stop. She ran to her mother's house, calling the names of her children even before she opened the door. They sat by the table with her mother, waiting, wide-eyed and still, and the grandmother held them while tears stood in her eyes and ran down her seamed face as she tried to speak. Ah, she is so old, Anna thought, and fell to her knees at her mother's feet, and went into her open arms, even as she reached out to grasp her babies and pull them close to her. "I'm home," she cried softly.

"I told them you would come back," the old mother said. "I told them."

And so the long journey was over.

CHAPTER TWO

My Father

MY FATHER FIRST CAME to Alaska in 1898. He was one of those thousands of white men who climbed up over the Chilkoot Pass that year of the gold rush, then came rafting down the Yukon from Canada, positive he would find gold in the next creek, or just around that big hill. He never did, but still he was luckier than most. Wandering the land looking for his bonanza, he came to know the country as well as any Native, and when he was really down on his luck he got a job with the Alaska Trading Company, hauling mail and passengers from Fort Gibbon to Louse Point, ninety miles down the river.

When the snow fell he drove a nine-dog team, and people who lived along the Yukon would wait for him to break trail, for everyone knew the mail had to go through.

My father was about twenty-five years old then, tough as the land and afraid of nothing.

I loved the stories he used to tell about those days. One winter he was hauling a wealthy Easterner all the way to Nome. When they came to the shelter cabin the first night, Dad thought it would be nice to offer his passenger a little something besides fried beans, so he opened a can of fruit for dessert. The Easterner looked at his tin plate with the remains of the beans still on it, then at the fruit, and finally said, "I would like to have a clean dish, please." Dad didn't say a word. He just took the plate outside where one of the dogs licked it clean as a whistle. Then he brought it back in and everybody was happy, especially the dog.

He was a good poker player. Once he cleaned out a game at Fort Gibbon, but the few hundred dollars he won chased him right out of Alaska. It seems the losers decided that they would get even with that Jim Huntington. They fed whiskey to an old Indian, which was against the law, until the poor buck was falling down drunk. Then they called in witnesses and said Dad had done it; they accused him of making a killing selling bootleg whiskey to the Native people. Soon the federal marshal at Fairbanks was on his way up the river with a warrant for Dad's arrest. He had just enough warning to beat the marshal out of town—and he kept going until he'd reached the coast at Valdez, nearly three hundred miles away, where he boarded a ship and eventually got back to his mother's house in Buffalo, New York.

But Alaska was in his blood. After he'd been away for two years, somebody told him that he couldn't be arrested for something that was supposed to have happened such a long time ago, so he kissed his mother good-bye, went straight back to Seattle, and got on the first boat headed north. This time he heard of a gold strike on the Koyukuk and staked a claim on Black Creek. He had to pack his supplies twenty miles over the mountains from Hughes, and build a giant fire to thaw the ground for his cabin. He never made much of his claim, just enough to keep him thinking that the pay streak was ten feet this side or the other from where he was digging. Whenever he went broke he ran freight up to Wiseman in a horse scow, leading the horse along the riverbank while a steerer tried to keep the scow from being spilled by the uprooted trees that came barreling downstream. Someone had said there was gold around Wiseman, and though it was sixty miles north of the Arctic Circle, the creeks were all staked and there were several saloons and six sporting women in the town.

By 1908 the country was filling up with miners. They were all over the streams back of Hughes, and it suddenly came to my father that if all these men persisted in digging for gold, he'd do better to supply them with shovels—and coffee and salt and anything else they needed — than he'd ever do working that stubborn land. So one spring morning he just walked off his claim and went into Hughes where, between the few dollars he'd saved and some he borrowed, he built a little trading post. By summer he was open for business.

That was the year he met my mother. Her Native village was only a hundred miles or so from Hughes, and Dad had been running trap lines through that country. He really liked the little Indian widow, but he did not believe in the Native style of marriage where a man and a woman say, "Okay, we're married," and that's it. So they waited until the Episcopal archdeacon came up the Koyukuk in

September and were married properly. They had a happy life together and five children—the older girls, Elsie and Ada, my brother Sidney and myself, and Marion, the baby. We were all born at Hughes, where we lived until 1919.

That year there was still another gold strike, this one at the mouth of the Hogatza River near my mother's people. Since the mines around Hughes seemed to be playing out, Dad decided to move his trading post down the Koyukuk to the new fields. With the help of some Indians, he pulled apart our cabin and store and built two big rafts with the logs. When the river was free of ice, we loaded aboard—kids, six dogs, and everything we owned—and drifted downstream. Dad picked out some nice high ground close to where the two rivers came together, and there he pitched the tent that was our home until he finished rebuilding the cabin and the store.

Those were my earliest memories. I was four years old that summer and trailed my father around like a pup. I remember standing alongside him on the riverbank when the steamer came by to take my two older sisters to the Anvik mission school, six hundred miles down the Yukon, and I tried to wave good-bye in exactly the free and easy way he did it. I remember the people who came to the store—my mother's brother Johnny, and the trappers with their stacks of furs to trade, and the rivermen who always stopped for what we called a cup of tea but was really a full meal.

And I remember being awakened one night by a terrific howl of pain. Our cabin had two stories and we kids slept upstairs, and though I was scared as could be, I came bumbling down the steps to see what was the matter. There sat poor Dad, hanging onto a chair with both hands, his mouth wide open. Mother had hold of one of his back teeth with a pair of pliers, pulling away with all the strength of her ninety pounds.

"Stop!" I yelled, and just then the tooth came out and Mother sailed back against the wall and Dad yelled again and I guess I thought the world was coming to an end.

Holding his jaw, Dad helped Mother up, then packed me back upstairs under one arm and put me into bed. "I believe you feel worse about this than I do," he said with a smile. I believe I did, too.

In the late spring, when the ice went out, Dad climbed into his riverboat with the new three-horsepower engine and set off for the Anvik mission to bring the girls home for the summer. It was lonely then, and my brother Sidney and I often sat on the bank staring down the winding Koyukuk, although it would be weeks before we saw that little green boat again. In the afternoon, Mother would come down to set out her fishnet. Then we'd mind the baby for her, standing on the bank and trying to see the silver flash of the first fish she caught. Sidney was seven then, I was five, and Marion not quite two.

Early one afternoon, whistle tooting and smoke heaving from her big red stack, the *Teddy H.*, first steamer of the season, came chugging around the bend of the river to tie up at our landing. The men left mail and supplies, then cast off, bound all the way to the mouth of the Yukon at the Bering Sea, with something for almost every post and village between. Sidney and I were glad to see them go; we weren't used to the tough-talking white men and their big, churning boat, and with Dad away there was something scary about their tromping around in the store.

That evening after supper it was so warm that we sat

outdoors, Mother sipping strong-smelling tea, and all of us watching the greening land. Far away, on the Zane Hills, you could still see winter's hand, rounded domes covered with snow and, lower down, the trees still skinny and bare. But close to the river here, you could almost reach out and touch summer. There were birds and new leaves on the bush, and the sky was bright blue. Some Native people who'd built cabins across the river from us had already moved down to their fishing camps, so the nearest people were the miners, twenty-five miles overland, and even farther by water. It was very nice.

Then Mother said she didn't feel well. She had eaten whitefish intestine for supper, a favorite Native tidbit, except that if it wasn't really fresh it could give you quite a stomachache. Suddenly her face was pasty white, and perspiration broke out on her forehead. When she got up to go back into the house it took her a long time, and she had to hold onto the wall for support. She lay down on the old bearskin couch, and Sidney brought little Marion in and then we stood there, frightened and not knowing what else to do.

When the sun started to go down, Mother looked up as though she didn't know where she was. "Give the baby some milk," she said. "Then go to sleep, all of you."

That made me feel better, hearing her talk and tell us what to do. I figured her stomachache would be gone in the morning. So I helped Sidney heat the condensed milk for Marion's bottle and fell asleep before he had even finished feeding it to her.

I was the first one awake in the morning. I remember lying there in the bed with the baby between Sidney and me and thinking that something was funny. I listened to the birds. I could even hear myself breathe. Then I realized that that was it: it was too quiet. Where were the sounds of Mother cooking breakfast downstairs? How come she hadn't wakened us to wash up?

I climbed out of bed and started downstairs. Near the bottom of the steps I stopped, for now I could see my mother. She was lying on the floor with just her head outside the partly opened door, as though she'd started for the privy and then gotten too tired to make it. She looked as though she was asleep, except that her face was on the ground and the mosquitoes were buzzing around it.

I went over to her, calling, "Mama! Mama!" I was positive she'd wake up when she heard me, but she never moved. When I went to shake her, the skin of her arm felt icy cold, though it was nice and warm in the house. I ran to the steps and screamed, "Sidney!" He came to the head of the stairs and I told him that Mother wouldn't get up. But my shouting had wakened the baby, and she was crying so hard that Sidney couldn't hear me. "Come down!" I pleaded.

He went back to get his overalls on and try to quiet the baby. Then he came down. He got to his knees by Mother and tried to call her, then shake her. But all that happened was that her face rolled around on the ground and got dirty, and I made him stop. I suppose I realized then that she was dead—I know Sidney did—but I think we both felt that as long as we didn't mention it, she might still wake up.

"Let's put her in the house before something eats her," Sidney said.

But small as she was, we didn't have the strength between us to budge her. Finally we covered her head and shoulders with a blanket. By now Marion was howling like a baby wildcat, and Sidney sent me to get her bottle while he made a fire to heat the milk. While I was upstairs I got dressed, then I came down to tell Sidney that the baby's diaper was one big mess. He told me to change it.

"I don't know how," I said.

He turned around from the stove where he was trying to get a blackened old log burning from a handful of birch-bark kindling. "I don't know anything about making breakfast," he said, "but I'm doing it." He could be awfully tough for seven.

I went back upstairs and took off the dirty diaper. It took me a long time to clean her up and get a dry one on her, especially since she was still crying for her bottle. Then I tried to lift her, piggyback, the way Sidney did, to carry her downstairs, but I wasn't big enough. "You'll have to walk down," I said, and took her hand. But she had never walked down the stairs before and was afraid. She whimpered and hung back. "Come on, Marion," I begged, near crying myself, "try! Sidney's trying to make us breakfast."

But it wasn't until Sidney showed her the warm bottle that she took hold of me, and half-sitting on each step, managed to get down. Then she curled up on the couch with the bottle and was happy. She never even noticed Mother laying there in the middle of the floor.

Sidney was stirring cornmeal in a pot of water, the way he'd seen Mother do. It kept getting thicker and thicker until finally he couldn't stir it anymore. Then it began to burn, so he said it was done and took it off the stove. It tasted terrible, but we ate it, even Marion. When we were finished we went outside, but we didn't feel like playing. Soon the dogs began to whine, and I was glad when Sidney said we'd have to water them, for that gave us something to do.

It took a long time. We had to pack the water up from the river, and all we could manage between us was half a pailful at a time. We kept going back and forth, and we took Marion with us. She kept falling down and crying, but she cried worse when we tried to leave her behind. Afterward, we gave her another bottle and changed her diaper. When she fell asleep, Sidney and I walked back to the bank and stood by the fishing skiff, turned over and drying in the sun.

"If we could drag the skiff down to the river we could drift along until we found somebody who'd go after Dad for us," Sidney said.

That scared me. The river ran awfully rough in the spring, and the boat looked much too big for little kids to handle. "Maybe somebody will come by soon," I said.

But Sidney shook his head, and we went back up to the house. When we got hungry, he warmed some leftover beans. Spread on a thick piece of bread, they tasted very good. Later, though, I noticed Sidney counting the tins of condensed milk in the cupboard and looking around for some other food. But everything there needed to be cooked, except for some more of the beans and about half a loaf of bread. We worried about how to get another milk tin open for Marion's next bottle—neither one of us could manage the can opener Mother used— and decided we'd try hitting it with a sharp stone. This finally worked, except that we spilled some of the milk, and Sidney got awfully mad. I tried to cheer him up by reminding him that we only had a few tins left anyhow, but he told me to shut up.

We ate the last of the beans for supper and went up to

bed even before the sun began going down—it was the time of year when the days were long. We kept waking up, though, because the mosquitoes were very bad, and with Mother stuck in the door the way she was there was nothing we could do to keep them out. Marion got all puffy with bites and cried and cried, and finally Sidney lit the kerosene lamp and we decided to take turns sitting up and shooing the mosquitoes off her. But that didn't work either because the light from the lamp drew them all the more and, anyhow, we kept dozing off. By the time the sun came up Marion's face was so swollen that she could barely open her eyes. She seemed to cry all day long, except when she had the bottle in her mouth, and Sidney and I were scared that she was going to die, too.

For breakfast we cut up the rest of the bread and soaked it in milk. It tasted good but there was a funny smell in the house and we were anxious to get outside. The dogs began to yip and pull on their chains when they saw us. Sidney said we'd have to get them some more water, so we put Marion in a shady place on the bank with her bottle and began filling the lard pail from the river and hauling it back up to where the dogs were staked. By the time we were finished the sun was hot and I was good and thirsty and I told Sidney I was going to drink the rest of the milk in Marion's bottle. He said I couldn't. "We have to save all the milk there is for her. She's a baby— she needs it."

"But I'm thirsty."

"Drink river water," he said. So I did.

Sidney kept eyeing the skiff. "If we could just get it in the water, we're sure to find somebody to help us," he said.

I still didn't want to, but I was hungry and lonesome for my dad. All the familiar things around the cabin and the landing had begun to look much bigger than they used to be—the boat, the trees back of the store, even the dogs. The whole world looked strange and big without anybody to run to when I was scared. Finally, when Sidney said we had to give the boat a try, I went over and began pulling on the transom with him.

Foot-by-foot we dragged it toward the bank through the softening ground. At the top, we rested for a long time, breathing hard and trying to figure out a way to get it turned right side up. Then, with both of us pushing from one side, we tipped it up on the gunwale and eased it down on the slope of the bank. Sidney ran around below to make sure it didn't begin to roll, and I was afraid it would fall on him. But somehow he got it turned bow down and it slid slowly toward the water. One last shove from the stern and it was launched—for about two minutes. Lying up in the sun all spring, the timbers had dried out and that boat shipped water so fast that if Sidney hadn't grabbed a line and made it fast to the landing we'd have lost it altogether.

He was very discouraged and hardly said anything all the rest of the day. By the afternoon there were no more clean diapers to put on Marion, so we took the dirty ones down to the river and washed them and hung them out on a pole to dry. We didn't go in the house until almost dark, and then we edged around Mother and pretended that we didn't notice the smell.

I fell asleep pretty soon, but I think Sidney was up most of the night. I know every time Marion's crying woke me, he'd be there sitting up alongside her, sometimes feeding her the bottle. When I opened my eyes in the morning, he was all dressed. "Let's go down and try to bail the boat," he said.

We dressed Marion and walked her down to the landing. Sidney took his shoes off and rolled up his pants, and standing in ankle-deep water in the boat, began to scoop with the lard pail. I stood on shore holding Marion. And little by little, the skiff sat up in the water; the timbers had soaked and swelled tight, and by noontime she looked trim and ready to go.

Sidney was proud and seemed to know exactly what had to be done. First we would pack some water up to the dogs, he said, then we'd load the boat with blankets, clean diapers, and the last of the milk, and we'd be all set to shove off. I was terribly hungry, but I didn't mention it because Sidney had so much else on his mind. Neither did I say anything about the wind that had blown up and was stirring white water in the river. I just did what he told me.

When everything was ready, I sat down in the bow holding the baby, and Sidney untied the line, pushing us far out into the current with the paddle. As soon as we were out where the dogs could see us, they set up a terrible howl, tearing against their chains and clawing at the ground. It was as though they knew we were headed for real trouble, and I was more scared than ever. Even Sidney, looking around at them over his shoulder, seemed worried. But all he said was, "They're hungry. We'll have to send food back for them."

Not that he could have turned back if he wanted to. The current must have been running a good five knots, and the wind pushed our bow from side to side, and hard as he swung that paddle, Sidney wasn't strong enough to do much more than steer around the worst of the shallows and deadheads. Spray splashed up in our faces, and Marion began to cry. Sidney hollered for me to give her a bottle, but

I couldn't take my eyes off that churning river. We hit a deadhead, scraped free, then hit another. Holding on to Marion, I couldn't keep my seat, so I set her, screaming and kicking, on a blanket in the bottom of the boat and crouched over her, clinging to the gunwale and praying that Sidney would turn us in to shore.

We came sweeping around a bend, and all at once the roar of shoal water was loud as thunder, I straightened my knees, stretching up until I saw it, foaming and angry and studded with gleaming rocks that seemed to reach clear across the river.

"Sidney!" I yelled.

He had already seen, but what could he do? If there was a channel through the shoal, he was much too close in to reach it, so he leaned on the paddle with all his might, trying to aim the skiff at the bank. I didn't see how we could make it. Even when he got the bow turned toward shore, the force of the current kept us running downriver broadside, and I was absolutely sure that we had to go smashing into those rocks. I took a good grip on the front of Marion's overalls—she was soaking wet now— and made up my mind that as soon as we capsized I'd grab for a rock with one hand and hang on to her with the other.

"The willows! The willows!" Sidney was screaming.

A little closer to shore now, the bow of the boat where I crouched was sweeping under a canopy of overhanging willow branches. I let go of the baby and stood, bracing my knees against the gunwale, and reached way out. Leaves and branches slid through my palms, bruising and burning them, but I didn't let go. I clenched with all the strength in both hands, and finally held fast, and the bow nosed in while the stern came pivoting around me, slamming into the bank so that Sidney was knocked off his feet. But we had come to a stop—not twenty feet from where those rocks would have dashed us to pieces.

For a long time I just hung on for dear life, feeling the river fighting to tug us free. I wasn't strong enough to hold with just one hand and pull closer with the other, so Sidney came forward and grabbed hold, too. And between us, we pulled the bow up onto the beach so he could jump out and tie us down.

We got Marion and the few supplies out, then sat on the bank, just resting while we gaped at the river. After a while we realized that the poor baby had never stopped crying. We gave her a cold bottle. That was the best we could do. She was sopping wet, but we didn't have anything dry to put on her. The blankets were soaked. So were the clean diapers. Soon Sidney said that we had to start back to the cabin.

"Through the bush?" I said. Dad had always warned us to stay out of the bush or we'd get lost. "We can't do that."

"What other way is there? I'll pack Marion. You bring the rest of the stuff."

He knelt down so Marion could climb up on his back and put her arms around his neck, and started off upriver while I still sat there worrying about the dangers of going into the bush. "Wait a minute!" I yelled, more scared of being left alone than anything else. I rolled the milk tins in the diapers, snatched up the blankets, and chased after him.

It was dark and tangly under the alders, and there always seemed to be threatening sounds behind us. I hated it worst when we stopped, but Sidney could only carry the baby for fifty feet or so before he had to put her down and rest. Once he tried to lift her onto my back. I fell down as soon as he let go. Then we begged her to walk, but she couldn't—her little legs were swollen with bites and the wet diaper was burning her raw—so we kept pushing on a little way at a time, trying to keep the sound of the river close on our left. Pretty soon it started to rain and the wind blew harder than ever, and I remember a sudden feeling of hot anger at my mother for being dead and letting all these bad things happen to me.

And then, way up ahead, we could hear the dogs barking. I don't know if they'd caught our scent or whether they were still agitated because we'd left them, but the racket they made was as sweet a sound as I've ever heard. We guided ourselves by it, and it grew louder and louder, and when we finally came out into the clearing I thought those dogs would tear loose of their chains in excitement and joy.

We were glad, too, but mostly we were tired. We had come only half a mile or so, but it had taken us three hours. We went up to the house to get out of the rain, but by now the smell was too much for us. It was the smell of death and we knew it and it reached all around the cabin.

"I'll go fix up the lean-to," Sidney said. "You wait here with Marion and I'll holler when it's ready."

But I wouldn't stay there alone, not when death was so real to me, so close, and so we all went back out into the rain together. I held the baby while Sidney raised a sort of canvas shelter that Mother used to clean fish under when the sun was very hot. We stretched the blankets out underneath and, wet as they were, we curled up in them, too worn out to care, and fell into exhausted sleep. The last thing I remembered was the sound of Marion sucking away on that cold bottle.

Sidney shook me awake. It must have been past midnight but in that far north country the sun was already coming up. "What's the matter?" I said, but he hushed me. I noticed that the rain had stopped and heard the dogs whining and was going to ask him again when finally I saw the bears.

There were three of them, black bears, a fat waddling mother and two cubs. They weren't thirty feet from the lean-to, between us and the dogs, sniffing and moving slowly over the wet ground, making a squishing sound as they went. I didn't breathe.

"If I could only get past them and turn the dogs loose," Sidney whispered.

I was terrified that he would leave Marion and me alone.

"Don't!" I begged. "Maybe they'll go away."

The she-bear turned her huge shaggy head toward us—she must have seen us!—and sloshed deliberately on. Very softly Sidney said, "If she starts this way, we'll each grab one of Marion's arms and run for the cabin."

I nodded. I was sitting up now and had got my feet under me and that made me feel a little braver. Then came the most terrible fear of all: what if the bears smelled Mother? What if they went up to the cabin and began eating her? I took a deep breath. If they did, I decided, I would go and turn the dogs loose. I would find a stick or something and try to chase them. I would do anything—even if they killed me—because nothing was worse than the thought of those bears tearing away at my poor dead mother.

I was about to lean close and tell all this to Sidney when the big she-bear turned up toward the woods, circling wide of the dogs, the cubs scurrying to keep up with her. In another moment, they had all blended into the dark bush. Soon Sidney lay back on his blanket, but I kept sitting there, just staring at that place where they'd disappeared. For a long time after that, I had it in my head that the mother bear had looked us all over before we were awake; she had seen Mother, and us kids alone in the lean-to, and she had decided that we were as helpless as her cubs would be if she were dead. And so she'd gone away without harming us. And the truth is, I'm not so sure I don't think the same thing now.

I didn't go back to sleep. I was so hungry that pains as sharp as knives tore through my stomach. I felt very weak. I asked Sidney if he was awake and he said yes. I told him how hungry I was.

"I'll go down to the river later and try to catch a fish with Mama's net."

He was just trying to shush me. I knew he couldn't catch a fish because it was very hard. And even if he did, he wouldn't know how to cook it. But what was the use of making him feel bad?

By the time the sun was up over the hills, the dogs had begun to moan and howl and wouldn't let up, not even after we brought them water. They kept walking slowly around their stakes, their tongues hanging down and a look on their faces when we came near them as though one of us was hiding a whole stack of dried salmon from them. It was now three days since they'd been fed anything but water, and although we didn't know it yet, worrying about them was to keep the three of us alive.

"We have to get them some food," Sidney said.

I looked at him as though he was out of his head. "What about us?"

"Us, too." He turned away and said, "We have to go in the store, Jimmy."

The store! I'd never even thought about it. There were two things Dad had drummed into us from the time we could understand him: we were never to go into the store alone, and we were never to touch anything in the store unless he gave it to us. But now ...

"Is there food in there?" I asked.

Sidney shrugged. "There must be something." He stood there a little longer, then went to make sure Marion was still asleep. "Come on," he said when he came back. And I ran after him, half-scared my father would suddenly appear to punish us, half-hoping he would—and so hungry that neither of those possibilities was as important as the food we might find.

Inside, it was cool and dark. Racks of furs and ammunition boxes were stacked in front of the counter. Hanging from the ridge poles were four big hams. They were raw and covered with a slimy mold that I'd seen Mother scrape off before she cooked a piece, but my mouth went all dry at the thought of chewing on a big juicy chunk.

Sidney got the butcher knife hanging on the back wall.

Then he climbed up on the counter and, reaching up as high as he could, sawed back and forth until—crash!—the ham went slamming down to the wood floor. We both looked at it. I thought: well, we're in for it now — then I said, "Come on, cut it up."

We squatted on the floor, jamming pieces of ham in our mouths as fast as Sidney could cut them, wiping some mold off and not worrying about the rest, and barely tasting any of it because we barely chewed any of it.

I don't know how long we might have stayed there

gorging ourselves if, after a while, we hadn't heard Marion crying. Full of guilt, we jumped up and tried to lift the ham. It was too heavy, so we grabbed the rope it had been hanging by and dragged it out of the store and over the damp ground to the lean-to. The dogs went crazy, thrashing and howling, but the first thing we did was cut little slivers for the baby. Then Sidney hacked off big chunks, and I threw them to the dogs, who snapped each one out of the air and bolted it down in a single gulp.

We fed them half the ham, then packed some water up for them. They were happy and, for a little while, so were we. Then Marion threw up all over the blankets, and Sidney and I were suddenly sick and barely made it outside before we heaved, too.

"I guess you're not supposed to eat it raw," he said sadly, and I wanted to cry because I was hungry all over again.

After that, we never ate another piece of that raw ham, no matter how hungry we got. Next day Sidney went back to the store and found a sack of hard candy, and we lived on that, and a can of beans from the counter that we finally pried open with the butcher knife. But more than once, just feeding the ham to the dogs, we'd gag on the slimy smell, and the memory of our great gluttony.

The days and nights began to get all mixed up. We got steadily weaker and slept a lot of the time, and it made no difference if the sun was up or not. Somewhere along the line we ran out of milk for the baby and had to put river water in her bottle. But she hardly cried any more. She'd just lay on the blanket, half asleep, never really awake. The bites on her body turned to angry red sores, and the mosquitoes never let up on her.

Once Sidney went up to the house to look for some food, but he didn't find any and he came back crying because Mother was in such bad shape. We didn't go near there anymore. In fact, we didn't go ten feet from the lean-to except to get water. We were very downhearted, and all we wanted to do was stay close together with the dogs watching over us. Sometimes at night we'd hear them barking at something, and we'd huddle close with Marion between us, too scared to look, just hoping that whatever it was would go away.

The time came when we weren't strong enough to pack any more water back for the dogs, but they only whimpered now and then, as if they understood that it wasn't our fault. We slept more and more, waking once in the middle of a pelting thunderstorm. We crawled farther back in the lean-to and listened to the rolling thunder, and Sidney said, "I hope Dad's not out on the river now."

I didn't think he was. I didn't think he was coming back at all. I had a feeling that one of these times we'd fall asleep and just not wake up any more, as Mother had done. When I told that to Sidney he said for me to shut up. Dad was coming back, he said. We just had to wait.

One day as I lay there dozing, it seemed to me that I was dreaming of a big boat and the crowd of white men who came barging off it. They were going to hit us for stealing candy from the store. Sidney was trying to tell them how hungry we'd been, but they wouldn't listen. They were dragging us back to the boat and the boat whistle blew with a terrific shriek—and I sat up on the blanket in a cold sweat.

There had been a boat whistle!

Sidney was already outside the lean-to, crouched

down on his hands and knees and staring down at the river. I crawled out beside him, and the whistle blew again, so piercing—loud that my ears hurt. The dogs were all up and howling at the sky. Drifting down in a wide swing toward our landing was the *Teddy H.*

I was terrified. I said, "Let's go hide."

Sidney looked at me, then back at the boat. He was scared, too, I could tell. I suppose we'd both gone a little wild. Still, he was older, and I think he would have been brave enough to stay if I hadn't run back and started pulling Marion to her feet. I was in a frenzy. Those men were scary enough when Mother or Dad were here. But now there was just us and we'd done so many bad things—taken stuff from the store and got the blankets all dirty. I was sure they'd come to punish us.

"Where'll we go?" Sidney said. He was still watching the *Teddy H.* as it nosed into shore. Now one of the men had jumped off the bow and was tying it down.

"Anyplace! In the store! Come on, help me with Marion." I guess he knew I meant to go, whether he did or not. He jumped up and, between us, we half-dragged, half-carried the baby past the yelping dogs and into the dim-lit store.

We edged deeper into the back, among the crates and cases. Hunkering down low, we found a little trapdoor in the floorboards and crawled under and in as far as we could go, barely able to move, too scared to breathe.

We could hear them wherever they went—they made so much noise. One yelled that the dogs were half crazy and soon another, up by the house, called out, "My God, the squaw's dead!" Then they said that we kids had to be around here somewhere, and they began looking all over.

Before long they were in the store. And as we lay there in the dark, wide-eyed and trembling in our nameless terror, Marion, who hadn't let out a peep for days, began to cry.

"Shhh!" I begged her, and tried to cover her mouth with my hand.

But it was too late. "Here!" one of them shouted. "They're over here somewhere, under the damned floor!"

But even when they shone a light through the floorboards and saw us, they couldn't get us out. They were too big to crawl in after us, and no matter how they pleaded, we huddled as far from their reach as we could get. "We won't hurt you," they said. "We'll take you to your father." But of course we knew they were lying.

Finally they got a crowbar and pried the boards up. They tried to lift Marion out first and Sidney and I sprang at them like a pair of wolverines, kicking at all the dark legs surrounding us, biting every hand that reached out. "Leave my sister alone!" I screamed. "Get away from my sister!"

But there were too many of them. Our strength gave out, and soon they held us with our arms pinned back. And still they kept saying that they weren't going to hurt us. "Poor crazy little kids," one of them said. "I don't know how they stayed alive."

They carried us back to the boat, and we were quiet until they tried to take Marion into a separate cabin. "Don't take her away!" Sidney hollered. "She's our sister! She's ours!"

So they took us all into the same cabin and stripped the stinking, filthy clothes off us and gave us a bath. They put some creamy stuff on Marion's bites and brought us cut-down pants and shirts. And nothing ever tasted so delicious as the warm mush they fed us. Then the captain came in. He was an old Eskimo named David Tobuk, and he said they were ready to bury our mother and we'd better come along.

They had dug a grave on the slope back up by the woods. Mother was all wrapped in canvas now and David Tobuk read a prayer while they lowered her in. Sidney held Marion tightly and we both began to cry because it was all so final. Once they covered Mother with dirt, we would never see her again.

As we walked back to the boat, the captain sent somebody to feed the dogs. He said, "We're going to turn back downriver and find your dad. He can't be many days behind us."

That cheered us up some. We felt foolish now for having been so afraid of these people. In the next days they became our friends, and we told them some of the things that had happened to us and how we had lived.

"Didn't you know that there was food all over that camp?" one of them said. "Cases of condensed milk and cornmeal in the store. Stacks of dried salmon in the cache."

"No," Sidney told him. "We didn't know."

Mother had a habit of marking an X on the calendar for every day that went by. The last X she made was on May 27, 1920, and the men from the *Teddy H.* found us June 10. So it was figured out that we had been alone in the wilderness for fourteen days. Everybody said it was a miracle—that we had survived on candy and a couple of cans of beans; that the bears hadn't got us, for they are wild with hunger in the spring. Years later, all over Alaska, people who heard my name would ask if I was one of the Huntington kids who had lived through that ordeal.

The real miracle was that the *Teddy H.* had stopped at

our place. They had nothing to leave for us on the return trip, and only the fact that someone had spotted the skiff downriver made them suspicious that something might be wrong. I doubt if we could have held out until Dad got back.

Six days after we'd left our camp, the boat whistle blew and everyone aboard seemed to grow very quiet. We went up on deck and saw Dad's green riverboat chugging upstream. The *Teddy H.* swung around, using just enough steam to hold it against the current, and David Tobuk hailed Dad from the starboard side. They talked for a while and Sidney and I hung back in a cabin door—now that Dad was actually here, we were a little jittery. Finally Dad and our sisters, Elsie and Ada, came aboard. The girls were crying, and Dad's shoulders slumped forward the way they did when he was very tired. Then we heard him call for us and we ran to him, and he put his arms around us real hard. Somebody brought Marion, and he kissed her and held us all. We had been very brave children, he said, very good.

"Dad," Sidney told him slowly, "we did do something real bad. We stole candy from the store, and a big ham."

"No, no!" Dad said, shaking his head and pulling us to him all the tighter. "That wasn't bad. That was..."

And then, at last, he began to cry and couldn't say any more. In a little while, they tied Dad's boat up behind the *Teddy H.* and we all went inside the cabin.

We were on our way home again.

CHAPTER THREE

Growing Up

THAT WAS A HARD and lonely summer for all of us, but mostly for Dad. He built a fence around Mother's grave and made a cross for it with her name printed on. And there he'd sit for long hours, looking empty-eyed at the river. He wouldn't even unpack supplies for the store. We weren't going to put in another winter in this place, he said, so unpacking would only be a waste of time. But he didn't say where we were going.

Early in August, the Episcopal archdeacon, Fred Drane, stopped to see us. He was making his annual mission up the river, holding services and baptizing babies in the villages and fish camps. He said prayers for Mother, and afterward we all sat out in front of the cabin and the Reverend Drane offered to take all five of us kids back to the Anvik mission, where Elsie and Ada had gone to school. You could see that this hurt Dad. He didn't answer, not even when the Reverend Drane asked how else he could manage, what he was planning to do. He just shrugged and sat there, looking without seeing, not saying a word.

In the late afternoon, my mother's mother, whom we called Old Mom, came up the river with some Natives in a poling boat. The men from the *Teddy H.* had brought her the bad news, and now she cried and cried as she held her grandchildren against her and put our hands to her mouth. In a little while, we all went back up to the grave, except for the Reverend Drane, who understood the Native ways. There, Old Mom built a fire and put biscuits and dried fish on it from the bag she was carrying. This was the Indian custom, to feed the spirit of the dead. She gave us some food, too, and while we ate she sang a Native prayer, nodding slowly while the tears ran down her lined old face.

We stayed until the fire went out. Then Old Mom told Dad that he had to get us kids out of this place, that it was bad for children to grow up in the wilderness without a mother. He didn't answer her, but when we got back to the cabin, he called the Reverend Drane aside and talked to him for a long time, and I knew that we would be going to the mission school.

When we woke in the morning, our clothes were already packed and loaded on the archdeacon's gas boat. After breakfast, Dad went to the store and got pretty handkerchiefs for each of the girls and two brand new jackknives for Sidney and me. He told us to be good. He said that Mr. Drane had promised to keep us all together, and that he would come to see us whenever he could. He carried the baby, and seemed not able to let her go when we got down to the landing. Mr. Drane had to take her from his arms, and then he just stood there all the time the boat backed into midstream and turned away. He was still standing there when the landing and the camp and the cabin disappeared from our sight behind a bend in the river.

Anvik is on the Yukon River, in the flat muskeg country of western Alaska, not too far from the Bering Sea. I didn't like it. Everybody there was good to us, but I just wasn't used to so many people or to the ways of the white man's world. I'd been born in the bush and lived there all my life, and I felt clumsy and shy among all those new faces and the painted buildings and plank sidewalks. I still do. But I had plenty to eat—although lots of times it was just navy beans—and I learned to read and write.

The best part of all was Dad's visit each spring. He didn't have the heart for running a trading post alone, so he'd been moving around the country, trapping some and digging for gold whenever someone told him about a promising streak. Sidney and I always begged him to take us along, but he kept saying that we needed an education. "Someday," he'd say. "When you're older." And so he'd give us each a dollar and leave again, and we'd go looking for something to buy that would last a long time. Usually it was peanut butter, which we'd take back to the dormitory and finish before the day was out.

In the third year I got sick and didn't get better for a long time. Some said I had TB, and they kept me in bed and fed me cod-liver oil by the bucket. Then I got whooping cough, and they had to send me to the railroad hospital in Anchorage. That was a very bad time. I was all alone and so sick that I was sure I'd cough my life away. One night I woke up hacking and gasping for breath, and when the nurse came I could hardly make her out: I'd ruptured a blood vessel and hemorrhaged into the left eyeball. For three months I was completely blind in that eye, and for a long time after that I had to wear colored glasses.

When I was well enough to go back to Anvik, I'd missed a whole year of school. I was like a stranger there, and the kids took to calling me One-Eye Jack. Naturally this led to some bloody battles, most of which I lost. I did better once I got my strength back. Anyway, they quit calling me One-Eye Jack, which was all I cared about. I didn't want them for friends.

In the winter of 1927, when I was twelve, my sister Ada came down with an attack of acute appendicitis. They tried to get her to the hospital in Fairbanks, but by the time they could get a plane in, it was too late. Ada died on the operating table. In the spring, when Dad came to see us, the hurt was still on his face. He looked thin and plain worn out.

"I'm going partners with old Charlie Swanson," he told us. "We got us a big poling boat with a kicker, and we're going up the Koyukuk to trap next winter."

Sidney and I had the old question on our minds, but we didn't ask it because you could see that Dad already had plenty to worry about. We had walked out toward the woods, just the three of us, and now he stopped and dug the heel of his boot into the thawing earth. "I figure it's time you boys were learning how to live off the country," he said softly. "Might be that I won't be around much longer to teach you. Think you'd like to come along with us this trip?"

Sidney and I almost busted open with excitement. We

said yes and danced around a little, for our dream had come true. Even better, Dad smiled as he watched us. He looked happier than we'd seen him in a long time.

So that was the end of my education. I'd gone through the third reader—which is more than most kids do in this part of the world—and now I was ready to start the learning that was to keep me going for the rest of my life: how to use what the land has to give you.

Dad stayed at Anvik until the ice was out of the river, then we said good-bye to Elsie and Marion, who were to go on with their schooling, and left for Nulato. Old Charlie was waiting there for us with the gas boat. He was a white man, all grizzled and gray, who never had much to say but sure knew how to tell you where you stood with him: ten minutes after we got there, while Dad was busy checking the boat, he dug around in his duffle bag and pulled out candy bars for Sidney and me.

We laid over a week in Nulato waiting for the steamer with all our winter supplies. We started loading as soon as they came. By the time we climbed aboard— with the seven dogs Dad had bought—that boat really sat down in the water. But there is no other way when you set off for a winter's trapping. If you forget something, or run out, you'd better be ready to do without because the nearest trading post might be a hundred and fifty miles away.

In a lot of ways, that was the best year of my life. The land was fresh and exciting to me then, the smells sharper, and there was a promise of game around each turn of the river. Everything was a challenge. Nothing came ready-made. And the people in Nulato were the last we were to see until the following spring.

Going upstream, we made twenty or thirty miles a

day, tying up to the bank each night and sleeping under the alders. Ducks and their young squatted in the sloughs, and took off in great wheeling clouds when they heard the chug of our motor. I counted thirty-four bears. One day we passed our old trading post, and a big blackie was ambling along on the slope near Mother's grave. You could only see the roofs of the buildings, at Hogatza, the grass stood that tall around them. We didn't stop.

On the eighth day we came to a nice sandbar below an open stretch of high ground. Dad said that looked like as good a place as any, so we tied up and pitched a tent on the bluff. I wanted to sit and just look around for a while—this was the place where we were going to spend a whole winter—but Dad said there was no time for sitting. And there wasn't. While Sidney and I unloaded the boat and staked the dogs out, Dad started clearing the land of brush. Then he took an ax into the woods and went right to work cutting logs for the cabin we'd have to have ready before snow fell. Meanwhile, Old Charlie was setting a couple of fishnets out in the river. The salmon were running now and they might not be tomorrow, and it took a lot of dried fish to feed a team of seven dogs all winter.

There seemed to be something to do every hour of every day. We had to build racks to dry the fish, and a cache ten feet off the ground to store meat. We went into the woods and picked gallons of wild blueberries, which Dad dumped in a big barrel along with a lot of sugar. This would be our fruit for the winter. Our biggest job was raising the cabin. We hauled logs from the woods and chinked them, and when it was tall enough we laid in the roof poles. Naturally we had no sheet iron for the roof, so we peeled spruce bark and laid that across the poles. On top of that went moss, then two feet of dirt, and that roof didn't leak a bit, not even in the hardest rain or when the snow thawed. We all worked, Sidney and I as hard as Dad and Old Charlie, and there was no such thing as a kid's job or a man's job. They were all the same—work that had to get done before winter—and I must have been the toughest twelve-year-old in the Territory that year.

We moved into the cabin around the middle of September. Our bunks were spruce boughs raised on poles, with lots of good grass for mattresses. Dad had brought a box of magazines, and when the days grew short we'd sit around the gas lamp reading them. Now we spent a lot of time building our sleighs and snowshoes. Dad showed Sidney and me how, once, then we were on our own. We fumbled and argued, but we got it done, and Dad said, "That's the way. Don't ever let anything stump you." The only bad part was that he made us take a bath every two weeks, and that was almost as bad as school.

When the ice began forming along the edges of the river, we ran the boat downstream to a slough and worked some logs under it so it wouldn't freeze to the ground. That took us all day, and on the way back Old Charlie joked about how we were really stuck here now and that there better be plenty of game for the pot. I fell asleep exhausted, as I did every night, happy as I'd ever been.

Next morning, when Dad called Sidney and me for breakfast, we shivered into our clothes and went to the water bucket to wash up. There, leaning against the cabin wall, stood two brand new .22 single-shot rifles. Our first rifles—our very own! For a second we just stared at them, then we yippeed loud enough to scare a deaf moose, Dad and Old Charlie grinning at us, and we begged for ammunition so we could try them out.

"Breakfast first," Dad said, and stood over us while we bolted down some mush. Then he gave us five rounds apiece, and out we tore, great and fearless hunters, on the track of a ferocious grizzly with enough meat on his rump to last through the winter. Of course we didn't have the patience to really look for any game—although there were rabbit tracks all over the place. Instead, we went out on the bank and shot at chunks of ice in the river. We never even came close.

We ran back to the cabin for more ammunition and Dad was waiting for us at the door. "Well, you've had your fun," he said, "and now we don't have any more ammunition to waste. From now on you're to quit treating those things like toys. They're supposed to bring in meat for the pot, and once you waste a shot you can never call it back, not even when you might need it real bad. Now go in and clean those rifles good."

It was a lesson I never forgot, like a lot of things I learned that winter. And next day when Sidney and I went out to hunt rabbits, I was hoping so hard I'd see one that they kept popping up in my imagination behind every tree and rock. Upriver a little way, we separated, Sidney heading into the bush and me following the beach around a little half-hidden slough. And at the far end I saw six ducks.

I dropped down, trying to shush the pounding of my heart, and crept up on them, foot by foot. They never saw me. They just sat there in the warm sun until I was close enough for a shot. I got up, scared to breathe, and tried to line one up.

But the gun swayed so badly that I couldn't even put the barrel on them, let alone the sight. Suddenly that rifle felt like a ton of lead in my hands, and the ducks got all blurry in my eyes and I just knew they'd spot me in another second and take off. Part of me wanted to yank off a shot and send them scurrying and get it over with. But the other part was remembering what Dad had said.

I lowered the rifle and looked around for a place where I could get down on one knee and still have a clear shot. Forcing myself not to rush, I got into position again. Now I was better braced and, holding my breath, I put a nice plump mallard in my sight and squeezed the trigger. The whole world seemed to explode, the ducks honking and beating their wings as they took to the air, the shot echoing all up and down the river. And as I stumbled to my feet and ran around the slough, I saw my mallard lying still on the water, not two feet from shore, shot neatly through the neck.

Oh, the feeling that was! Holding my prize out in front of me, running home as though the frozen ground was made of rubber and bounced me along in ten-foot strides! What would I say when I got there? How should I look? And finally bursting into the cabin and forgetting everything, stammering, looking dumbly at the duck, then at Dad and Old Charlie. And Dad, so proud he couldn't hide it, saying, "What've you got there, son?"

And finding my voice at last. "It's a duck, Dad. Meat for the pot."

When the river froze and the snow fell, we began scouting the bush for fur signs. We walked eight or ten miles a day, taking a different route each time so we'd know our way around the country, and saw plenty of mink and fox tracks. Dad said it looked good. Then we had to cut dog trails to the places where we planned to set out with the trap lines. This was hard work, chopping trees and hacking the brush out of the way, and it always felt good to stop for some lunch and sip tea by the fire while Dad and Old Charlie talked about trapping and the old days in Alaska.

When there was enough snow on the ground, we hooked the dogs into two teams and began taking them out on the trail to toughen them up. They'd been tied down for so long that they ran as though we were whipping them, jerking the sleds wildly, their breath steaming on the frosty air as they yipped and pulled in their harness. Once, early on, when we were still testing different kinds of traps, we caught a mink and brought it back, although you could see that the pelt wasn't prime yet. I guess we shouldn't have because when Old Charlie was skinning him out, he cut the scent bag by accident and stunk us all out of the house.

By November first, all the traps were set. A week later we split into two teams, Old Charlie and I taking three dogs, Dad and Sidney the other four, and we went out to see how we'd done. For a first set, we hadn't done badly at all. From the two trap lines, each about six miles long, we brought back five mink, two foxes and a lynx, and we all had a busy night skinning.

The winter flew by. Every few days, we'd take off to check the traps, and whenever the catch thinned out we'd move them to a new place. The pile of skins in the cache grew higher and higher. Dad and Old Charlie were mighty happy, for the price of fur was way up in that year of 1928, and since they owed no one a cent, everything they made could go into next year's grubstake. Meanwhile we had plenty to eat. Sidney and I brought in our share of rabbits, and once Old Charlie shot a fair-sized bear that kept us in soup and meat for a long time.

Around Christmastime it got good and cold. The

thermometer outside our front door dropped to sixty-five below zero and stayed there for more than a month. If the sun sneaked out during the few hours of daylight, it might warm up to minus forty-five, but the sun seldom sneaked out. Weather like that is too tough to travel in, so we stayed close to the cabin. We read that stack of magazines so hard that we knew each one by heart, and we cleaned our rifles until you could practically see your reflection when you looked in the chamber. Old Charlie taught Sidney and me how to make a rabbit snare, which didn't exactly thrill us: snares saved ammunition, but hunting was about the only fun we had during those freezing cold weeks.

Late in January it began snowing, and it didn't stop until it dumped three feet on top of the old fall. The cold spell was over, but now we had to go out and break trail to the trap lines and dig up our catch. That took us ten days but it was sure worth it: we had caught thirty-six foxes, seventeen mink, and twenty lynx.

By this time, Sidney and I could handle the dog teams well enough to run the trap lines alone. It was on one of those trips that I foolishly followed a marten track and got into serious trouble, proving that there are some things you can only learn the hard way.

It was a fine morning and when I spotted the tracks I thought what a nice surprise it would be if I came home with a good thick marten pelt. So I put on my snowshoes and staked the dogs and took off, positive I would catch up with the marten before long, as I knew they moved very slowly over the snow. The thing is, I knew just enough to foul me up: the part I hadn't learned was that when the snow is deep, a marten will burrow into it as soon as he sniffs danger, and you can turn blue waiting for him to come out. That's what happened to me. I shuffled along in his tracks for more than two hours, around a hill and along a creek that bent back on itself, and just as I caught sight of him—whoosh!—he dove into the snow and that was that.

I hung around there for a little while—I sure wanted that skin—but when the sun started down I decided I'd better head back. Thinking to save time, I crossed the creek and went up over the top of the hill. Only it turned out to be the wrong hill, and after I'd followed a long, bare ridge for a mile or more, I knew I was pretty well lost. What worried me most was getting caught out there by darkness. I had no food, nor anything to make a fire with, and one night in the open can be a long time in that country. I was pushing on, straining to see a familiar landmark, when suddenly a wolf showed up on the ridgeline, thirty feet in front of me.

At that range, the sight of a timber wolf—a big, dirty-gray creature, teeth grinning in a bullet-shaped muzzle— is enough to stop you in your tracks. As a matter of fact, the real temptation is to turn around and run. And in the instant that I saw the thing, I did break stride—then forced myself to keep going. For there sprang into my mind the two rules Dad had given me about wolves: when you see one, look for others, for mostly they travel in packs; and when you show them you're afraid, you give them the courage to attack.

There was certainly truth in the first part. As I moved skittishly ahead, feeling the cold sweat of fear gathering under my parka, I could see that there were at least twenty other wolves waiting for the leader, the one in my path, to make his move. They crouched on the high ground to my left, and ranged beneath the crest of the ridge on the right, and they never took their shining black eyes off me.

Without raising my rifle, I kept the muzzle pointed at the big brute in front of me, and my finger circled the trigger. Now we were so close that I could hear his agitated breathing and I know he heard mine. I could surely kill him at this range, but pumping away with a single-shot rifle, I wouldn't get many rounds off if the rest of them came at me. So I just kept walking and, at the last instant, the wolf gave ground, grudgingly, snarling at my heels as I edged past him.

But he wasn't finished with me, oh, no. He dropped back ten feet or so and began following in my tracks, panting, his big head swinging from side to side. And as he moved after me, so did the pack, swarming around on both sides of the ridge, crowding nearer as their leader got braver and closed the gap between us. I knew it couldn't go on this way much longer. Now that my back was to him, he was full of fight, barking at my heels and running at me in frenzied little dashes that stopped just short of my ankles. Soon—next time or the time after—he wouldn't stop. And once he hit me I'd go down—he outweighed me by thirty pounds - and the instant I was on the ground the others would close in and that would be that. And so, thinking the whole thing through and realizing that it was suicide to stop and impossible to run, I decided I'd better have it out with them then and there, while I was still on my feet. I swung back from the waist and at pointblank range put a .22 slug right between the leader's eyes.

That's when I really learned about wolves, how cruel and cowardly they are. The sound of the shot stunned them for a moment. Then, instead of coming at me, they ran at the safer prey—their dead leader. Inflamed and half-crazy, they fell on his body and began tearing it to pieces. I never stopped and, except for that one quick look, I didn't turn around.

In a little while I came down off the ridge and doubled back toward the creek. When I found my old tracks, I did what I should have done in the first place: followed them back in the direction I'd come from, retracing my steps over all that wandering way the marten had led me. It was just about dark when I finally reached the sled. Tired and mighty thankful, I tumbled in and hollered for those dogs to take me home.

The days started to get longer—spring was coming. To kill time, Sidney figured out how to make a violin, copying a picture in one of the magazines. He hollowed out a piece of tree stump for the box, used wire cable for the strings and a willow branch rubbed with spruce pitch for the bow. It didn't sound too bad, either. Of course we didn't know the first thing about playing a tune, but it was sort of nice to saw away on the thing and make something that sounded like music.

I kept looking at a picture of a guitar, and pretty soon I decided I had to have one. There was no tree around big enough for the box, so I cut out a gasoline can, carved the arm from a piece of birch and put them together with some sawed-off ten-penny nails. The thing would only take two strands of cable for the strings, but since I didn't know what I was doing anyhow, one string would have been plenty. Every day that it was warm, Sidney and I would go down by the bank to "play" our "instruments," and as far as we were concerned, finer music had never been made. But that was only our opinion. One morning Dad came down to look at the ice in the river and said he guessed it might go out any day.

"How come?" I asked. It was early spring, and the ice looked solid as rock.

"With all that noise you're making, I don't see how it could stand to stay much longer," Dad said.

One day Old Charlie came in and announced that something had been stealing his fish. He thought it might be a bear, but couldn't tell for sure because we'd all been tromping through the snow around the fish racks and you couldn't see a track. We moved the dogs close to the racks and, sure enough, that night they set up a terrific racket. But by the time we ran out, the bear, or whatever it was, had gone—and taken another line of fish with him. The dogs hadn't scared him one bit. This went on for three nights, and Old Charlie kept getting madder and madder, mostly because of the nerve of the thing, but also because we were running pretty low on fish by this time. On the fourth night, Old Charlie said he was going to take his rifle and sit outside, even if it took until daybreak.

Dad had a better idea: "Why not let the kids make a big snare trap? Set it about three feet off the ground, and if it's a blackie, he should put his neck right through it."

Sidney and I went to work. We used quarter-inch cable, and put the trap at the edge of the brush where it came closest to the fish racks, and at just the right height. Then we all went off to bed. This time our visitor didn't come until the sky was beginning to lighten. As soon as we heard the dogs, we jumped into our boots, Old Charlie grabbing the .30-.30 as we rushed outside. At first all you could see was what looked like a windstorm in the willows—they were really flying around. Then, in the middle of all the action, we made out a thrashing mountain of brown fur. Old Charlie didn't waste any time. He pumped two shots into it, and suddenly everything was quiet. But when I started running toward the brush, Dad stopped me:

"Take it easy, son! You want to be sure with a brown bear."

A brown bear! Sidney and I had caught a brown bear in our snare! The biggest animal in Alaska—the biggest meat-eater in the world, I guess. Because of his huge size, we'd snared him, not by the neck, but by the front paw—he'd gone to shove the trap aside and got caught.

Old Charlie moved up and put another shot in his head, then we all crowded close. That bear looked enormous to me, one of his paws as big around as my whole body. Dad said he'd weigh in at a thousand pounds, which is a lot of brown bear. And it's a good thing Old Charlie hadn't wasted any time with the rifle: the bear had fought the cable so hard that he'd unraveled it in two places and would have busted free in another minute, and mad at the world. We spent the morning skinning him out, but he smelt so strongly of fish that none of us would touch the meat. The dogs liked it, though.

Waiting for the ice to go out, we decided to build a poling boat. We went back up on the hill where the timber was tall and broad around and we built a saw pit. Then we chopped down a good straight spruce, peeled it, and whipsawed the planks we'd need. In a couple of weeks we had a fine poling boat. Dad said it would be a big help when we loaded up to take our skins downriver.

Actually, we were going to need it long before then — and it was a good thing for all of us that we had it. Well into May there was still a lot of snow on the ground and on the river ice, and that was a bad sign. Carrying all that snow, there was every chance that the ice would jam when it finally went out, and that the river would flood.

One afternoon, we heard a great rumble upstream. It was an angry sound, like thunder rolling at you out of the sky. Dad and Old Charlie, who knew right away what it was, ran for the bank, and Sidney and I followed. Half a mile up the river, a blue-white wall of ice had been shoved fifty feet out of the water, massive chunks under terrific pressure, groaning against one another as they were forced up from a winter-long lock on the river. The ice was going out, and it was going fast.

"Get everything out of the cabin," Dad said sharply. "Put what you can on the roof. Put the rest in the cache."

We ran. And while we packed blankets and cans of beans out, Dad and Old Charlie tied the poling boat to the cabin and began piling stuff into it. And even as we worked, the ice came thundering down the river past us, reaching high above our heads, and geysers of water shot up over the bank. We knew we were in for it. The dogs whined and pulled on their chains, and Old Charlie undid them two at a time and tied them in the boat. Then the ice jammed up just below the cabin, a heaving dam building from bank to bank, and the river came tearing over the land in a wild rush.

"Into the boat!" Dad yelled, and Sidney and I jumped in from the roof of the cabin and hung on for dear life.

The water surged under us, lifting us, and fingered out toward the woods. It swirled around under the cache and knocked over the fish racks, and still it kept rising. Dad clung to the line, the boat pitching madly, until we were level with the top of the cabin door. Then he cut loose and shoved us into that wild torrent, he and Old Charlie paddling toward the woods for all they were worth. Chunks of ice slammed against us, and the dogs howled, and Sidney and I crouched down on trembling knees and didn't look at each other.

Dad was steering for the winter trail back of our clearing, it was the only open area in all that drowned land for as far as we could see. Trees thrust just-budding crowns out of the wild water, and caught masses of ice in their branches and in grinding whirlpools around them. Dad held to the trail—it seemed so crazy to be riding among the treetops—and pushed on by the outpouring river, we made it back to the hills that once looked down on all that land and were now lonely little islands poking up out of the great flood.

We stayed there for eight days, living off the few supplies we'd brought along, and sleeping on the cold ground. Old Charlie wanted to take the boat back to the cabin and get some more stuff, but Dad said it was too dangerous. Then the jam broke and the water went down and we picked our way back. The few things left in the cabin were a soggy, silty mess. Of all the stuff we'd stashed on the roof, only the guitar and fiddle and a case of navy beans were left. Sick at heart, we walked to the cache—and it was gone, gone with our meat and the whole stack of furs. Gone was a whole winter's work.

Dad and Old Charlie didn't say a word. They just walked around a little, not coming close to each other. Then they went back to the cabin.

It took three days for the ice to clear out of the river. Then it was safe for us to paddle downstream to the slough where we'd propped the gas boat the autumn before. No one said much about it, but we were worried that it might have been damaged by the flood. The slough was still choked with ice when we got there. Uprooted trees floated in the shallow water, and the beach looked as though it had been torn by a great windstorm. And there was not a single sign of the gas boat. It was gone, too.

That night, Dad and Old Charlie talked the whole thing over and made some tough decisions. We had to try and find the gas boat and, somehow, we had to put together enough of an outfit to see us through the next winter. Since we couldn't all fit in the poling boat on the three hundred-and-fifty-mile trip down to the Yukon, Old Charlie volunteered to stay behind with the dogs. He'd live off the land until we got back, he said, and spend the time tidying up the cabin and building a new cache and racks. It was the bravest thing I ever saw a man do. When you've spent a year trapping, coming in out of the bush becomes an obsession: you dream about the taste of store food and the warm feeling of swapping stories with the other men, and I sure felt sorry for Old Charlie when Dad and Sidney and I pushed off from the bank and left him standing there, all alone.

Not that we had an easy job. We'd have to poke into every slough and stop at every village looking for the gas boat. And though we had no money and nothing to trade, still we'd have to bring back a grubstake or face a mighty lean winter. One thing we decided on: to go on down below Nulato and do some fishing so we wouldn't have to pay for dog food.

After rowing all day, we got our first good break. A fur trader tied up near the mouth of the Hogatza told Dad he'd heard that a badly damaged gas boat had been pulled off the ice by some Natives at Koyukuk Station. He said he was headed that way and would take us along. We loaded our stuff aboard and tied the poling boat on behind and shoved off. Dad and the trader took turns steering, and since there is practically no darkness that time of year, we made it to the Yukon in three days. Next morning, we found the men who had beached our boat. Dad told them he had no money and promised to come back and pay them the next spring. But they said they didn't want any pay; they only hoped he could fix the boat up. Alaska used to be that way.

That old boat looked in sad shape. The cabin had been knocked off and a big hole punched in the side, and the decks were awash with a foot of muck. To me, it seemed beyond repair. But Dad went right to work shoveling the mud out, and Sidney and I pitched in. When we'd made a temporary patch for the hole, we dragged it into the water and paddled downriver to Nulato, twenty miles away, where we hoped to get the old Model T motor running again.

People in Nulato were glad to see us again, and felt sorry when Dad told them about our hard luck. It seemed that all the would-be mechanics in the place were down at the landing trying to help us get that motor started. But even after it was all cleaned up, the best they could do was get two cylinders working, and no matter what they tried, the other two wouldn't kick over. For three days the men took turns at it, but no one could figure out what was wrong. Once I asked Dad if he thought it might be out of time, but he told me to hush; these men knew all there was to know about motors.

But I couldn't get it out of my head. I kept watching them work, wanting to change those spark-plug wires so badly it hurt, but scared to open my mouth. Finally, one of the men looked up and, teasing, asked me if I knew what the trouble was. It came blurting out of me like water freed by a broken beaver dam: "I think it's out of time. I think if you change the plug wires—put number one where number four is—I think it'll work."

He grinned at me. "Go ahead, son, try it. You can't do any worse than us experts."

Dad, who had been talking to one of the men, came over to watch. My fingers felt like claws as I fumbled those wires around. But when it was done and they cranked the motor, it took off like a clock, and those men slapped their knees and laughed and laughed. And Dad put his arm around my shoulders and squeezed real hard. After that, and to this very day, people would come get me to fix their engines. Sometimes they'd give me a dollar and sometimes not, but it never really mattered. I just like to work on engines.

Sidney and I wanted to stay around the village and have some fun, but the salmon were running and Dad said we had to get going. We spent nearly a week building a fish wheel, which is a rig that sits in the water with eight or ten scoop nets poking out past the rim. The current turns it, like a windmill, and the nets scoop up the fish going by and dump them in a big trough. When it was finished, we stuck it out in front, tied the poling boat behind, and went downriver about twelve miles to a nice camp. We pitched a tent there and spent the next couple of days building racks and a smokehouse.

Then the salmon hit. I had never seen anything like it, the way they came up that river like a red tide, so thick it seemed you could cross on their backs, thrashing for swimming room, jumping high out of the water to clear the deadheads, fighting with their last strength to get back to the lakes where they were spawned, to lay their own eggs there, and to die. Each dip of the wheel brought up four or five fish, and with all three of us working as hard as we could, we were barely cutting and hanging them as fast as the wheel was catching them.

One day, when we'd been there about a week, Pop Russell, the trader from Nulato, pulled in. He and Dad just visited for a while, then he sort of cleared his throat and said he'd been thinking about us and how we were going to make out come winter. He wanted to stake us to an outfit—"Strictly business!" he said: he ran a big string of dogs, and if we'd bring him a load of dried fish, he'd consider that a down payment. We could settle up when we came down with our furs the following spring. Dad reached over and shook Pop Russell's hand hard, and smiling the way he hadn't smiled since breakup. He said to Sidney and me, "Boys, we're in business again!"

Now we really worked! The smokehouse was going night and day, and when the racks were full we built more. By the first of August we had Pop's fish all bundled and three thousand for our own dogs. We loaded up and went back to Nulato, where Dad said that we'd put in a hard year and deserved a little fun. "I'll be tied up here a week or so putting the outfit together, so you two find some boys your own age and have a good time."

We sure did. At first I was ashamed because my clothes were so raggedy, but when I saw that the other kids in the village weren't much better off, I never gave it another thought. We swam in the river and played a sort of soccer game with a caribou-hide ball, as many on each team as wanted to play, with no time limit and no holds barred. That game will sure keep a person in shape. A young Native who'd been to school in Anchorage taught Sidney and me to pick out a couple of tunes on our "instruments," and the people would gather around us in the evening and clap their hands and sing. We slept in different houses—everybody made us welcome—and it got so that I liked town living pretty well. I said to Dad: "People aren't too bad, once you get to know them."

The chill of autumn was in the air by the time we left. Dad had built a new pilothouse on the gas boat, so we slept aboard that first night. When I woke up, I felt like jumping clear out of my skin—my body itched from a million fierce little prickles and bites. Sidney was already up and scratching madly, and Dad had gone out on deck and torn off all his clothes. "Get out here, you two!" he hollered, and we hustled on deck where he made us strip down bare. I'd never seen him so mad. "People aren't too bad, eh?" he kept muttering. "They're lousy. That's what they are!"

And finally Sidney and I got the drift of what he was saying: sleeping around from cabin to cabin, we'd collected a fine assortment of lice. Now we stood shivering in the cold air, naked as the day we were born, while Dad dug a couple of quarts of coal oil out of the kit. Then we went ashore and he poured it over our heads. "Rub it in good!" he said. "Everyplace!" And when that was done he ordered us into the river.

"Oh, no!" we begged. The water was so cold that ice was already forming along the shore, but Dad wouldn't take no for an answer.

"In!" he roared, and the three of us went tiptoeing into that frigid water, duck bumps, chattering teeth, and all.

Only when we'd scrubbed ourselves raw would he let us back on the boat. We put on some clean clothes—boy, did that feel good!—and left the old ones right where we'd thrown them on the beach. Those lice must have missed the nice warm bed we'd made for them, but I could still imagine them biting me a week later.

Dad let Sidney and me do most of the steering going back upriver. Not long after we passed the Huslia River, the motor began to knock and smoke badly. As soon as it cooled, we tore it down and found that the number four connecting-rod bearing was burned out. We didn't have a spare, and Dad was worried that if we horsed around trying to get one up from Nulato the ice would catch us before we made it back home. I looked at that bearing for a long time, then said I thought I could make a new one from the liner. Dad shrugged, as if to say he'd try anything, and I went to work. Four hours later I had it fitted on the crankshaft, and when we kicked the motor in, it ran as smoothly as ever. "You might amount to something someday," Dad said with a smile.

We stopped at Hogatza to clean Mother's grave. As we were leaving, I spotted the old three-horsepower outboard almost hidden by grass down at the landing. It was all rusted and beat up, but I asked Dad if I could take it. He said sure, although it wasn't worth anything. From then on, I worked on it every spare minute I got, even on the trip upriver. I was to fiddle with that thing for a whole month before I got it to kick over. Then, all excited, I stuck it on the poling boat and went chugging upriver. I couldn't have gone more than a mile before it spluttered and smoked and conked out altogether. It would never run again either, so all I got for my work was a mile ride. But I sure learned a lot.

We were ten days making it back to camp. When we

pulled around the last bend, there stood Old Charlie on the bank, waiting, just as if we'd only gone downriver a couple of miles to do a little fishing. Gosh, we were glad to see him! We pumped his hand, and the three of us tried to tell him everything that had happened, all at once. And Old Charlie just stood there nodding, as though he never doubted that we would do all we'd set out to do— find the gas boat, bring back fish for the dogs and an outfit for winter. And when we finally ran out of breath, he said, calm as could be, "I've been scouting the hills. Signs look pretty good."

They went too fast, those years. Little by little things got more complicated, and the people I loved best dropped out of my life. Old Mom was first to go. One spring a Native came poling up the river to tell us that she was failing and wanted to see her grandsons one more time. Dad took Sidney and me right down to Rock Island Point where she lived. We stopped in Hughes to buy her a blanket, and when she saw it tears came to her eyes and she couldn't talk. Finally she said that she would have them put that blanket in her coffin, so she would have it always. Then she gave Sidney and me a pair of fur boots and moose skin mittens that she'd made. She held our hands to her mouth for a long time before we left, telling us to be good boys and always to remember our mother. We stopped in Rock Island Point again on our way back from Nulato that summer, but she had already died.

By the 1930s, the price of furs had dropped to practically nothing. Pop Russell wouldn't even take them in trade—he'd send them outside and give us whatever they brought, which wasn't much. People said that they were having a depression in the States, and that no one could afford to buy furs anymore.

Still we got along. There was always meat for the pot, and the cabin stayed snug and warm on the coldest nights. We had no rent to pay, no fancy clothes to buy. We had no use for a clock. We lived off the land, and the land was the only thing we had to answer to. As long as we stayed tough and smart, we'd make out.

But then everything seemed to go wrong. Dad got sick with TB, and though he tried to stick it out with us, taking care of the cabin and doing the cooking while we ran the trap lines, you could see him get weaker every day. Finally he went to live in the pioneers' home in Sitka where he got good medical care and everything he needed. "I'll be back," he said to Sidney and me when we brought him to Nulato to catch the steamboat. "As soon as I'm better we'll be together again. Maybe we can raise a little money and start up a trading post somewhere. A trapper's life is too hard."

Sure, we told him, whatever he wanted to do. But we knew he'd never be back, and we were brokenhearted because we loved him so much.

We trapped together for another couple of years, Sidney, Old Charlie, and I, and then the trail got to be too much for Old Charlie, too. He went downriver looking for wages, but times were worse than ever, and all the way to Fairbanks he couldn't find work. We heard that he died there, some said of starvation.

That same year—it was 1932—Sidney met a Native girl at Koyukuk Station and wanted to get married. I told him to go ahead, not to worry about me. He said we could still go trapping together, the three of us, but I knew better than that. So after the wedding I wished him luck and took off. I was sixteen and on my own.

ON THE EDGE OF NOWHERE

CHAPTER FOUR

Living on the Land

SIDNEY AND I SPLIT the outfit fifty-fifty—guns, traps, and dogs. He took the old gas boat and I took the one we had built the year before, a big, broad-beamed job that we called the Ark. I was supposed to get the cabin, but all kinds of trappers had moved into that country, cheechakos mostly, and that was too much company for me. So I packed my gear up to the old trading post at Hogatza. The fur signs were good there, and it didn't take much to put the store in shape for living. I didn't even have to chop firewood: I just tore the old cabin down and burned that.

There were a lot of geese that year, and I ate well. Of course it's against the law to shoot geese, but any time a white man who's never set foot out of Juneau or Fairbanks makes a law for the North country, you can be pretty sure it will be a foolish one. For the Native people, getting enough to eat is mostly what life is all about. They have always shot geese, in season and out, and so have I. I have never taken more than I could eat in a few days. I have never killed any game for "sport," only to bring in meat for the pot or to defend myself.

People say that with all the wildlife in Alaska no one should ever go hungry, but they do. In a dry year, animals will move a hundred miles or more, and that's a long way to be tracking game. And even when conditions are just right, nature has ways of protecting its creatures. They're smart. Every hunt is a contest, with no guarantee that man is going to win out.

Take beaver. They're nice and fat in the winter and make a wonderful meal. But if you get one, you've really earned that meal. Beavers build elaborate rooms and tunnels under the ice, and it takes a pen set, a kind of trap, and a lot of hard work to trap them. But when you're hungry and go hacking through the ice looking for food, chances are they'll slip away down an escape tunnel while you're freezing on the bank and wondering where they are. If you shoot one it had better be a big one: the others will stay down until the ice is out of the river.

A moose will keep you in meat for a long time, but that's a problem in itself. One day that first year I was alone, before the ice had come in, I was nine or ten miles upriver in a canoe when I heard a moose calling. I pulled in by the bank and, after a little while, I answered him. Pretty soon something moved in the brush up ahead and this big buck stepped out on a sandbar right in front of me, looking around as though he owned the whole world. I dropped him with one shot, then paddled up to where he lay, the biggest darn moose I'd ever seen in my life. The more I looked at him the bigger he got, and I knew I'd have my work cut out for me hauling him back to the cabin. When I got his head cut off, I could almost straighten up between his horn spread: it would have been a prize for some trophy hunter from the South 48, but it was a pain in the neck to me.

It took me five hours to skin that thing out, and then I couldn't load it in the canoe without swamping. Finally I cut two logs for outriggers and fastened the canoe between and drifted on home. By the time I'd got it packed up to the cabin and hung, I'd sworn that if I ever shot another big moose again he'd have to be knocking at my front door.

As it turned out, all the meat was put to good use. Next morning two white men came downriver in a gas boat. They said they were taking the census, which they explained meant counting all the people in Alaska, and asked me a lot of questions. They kept looking at the moose meat, so I told them to take what they wanted. I gave them tea and, when they were getting ready to leave, asked if they would haul a quarter of the moose down to my Uncle Hog River Johnny at Cutoff. I offered them a can of gas for their trouble, but they said it was no trouble. I watched for a long time as they pulled away, wondering why anyone would want to know how many people there were in Alaska. Next thing they'd be delivering mail in the winter!

Uncle Johnny was sure glad to have that meat. He was still talking about it when I took the dogs down to Cutoff to visit him at Christmastime. Next fall, he said, he was going to teach me how to hunt bear, and that was as good an exchange as I've ever made.

Bear are worth all the trouble it takes to pack them

home. The meat is delicious, and the ribs make a good, thick soup. The only thing is, you have to know what you're doing or the bear you're stalking may come up behind and tap you on the shoulder—which would leave you short one shoulder.

No two bears are alike. The brown bear is smartest, the grizzly meanest, and the blackie most unpredictable. Sometimes you can pass as close as twenty feet upwind of a black bear and he won't pay the slightest attention. Another time he'll track you for miles. Once I was paddling down the river about thirty feet from shore, when a blackie came charging down the bank, jumped in and came after me, thrashing through that water like a hippopotamus. I really leaned on that paddle!

Late one afternoon, while I was setting traps in a little thicket, I heard a terrific roar and looked up just in time to see a cow moose galloping right at me. I yelled for all I was worth and the moose swerved out, missing me by inches. Right behind her came a brownie, in full charge. I dived out of his way—and kept right on going back to my camp while he was busy polishing off that moose. Next day, when I went back to my traps, I took a different route, walking way around to come out at the thicket on the downwind side. And sure enough, there stood the brownie, waiting for me alongside my trail: he'd had a whiff of me as he tore by the day before, and caught the same man-smell from the traps, so he figured I'd be back. He'd have been all over me, too, and before I ever saw him, if I'd come back the old way. I sure admired his brains, and I didn't really need the meat. But I did have to get to my traps, so I shot him.

The best bear hunting is in the late fall, when they hole up in their dens. That time of year you can get five gallons of lard from a good bear, besides the meat, and that means a lot in the wilderness. Of course you can't just walk along poking into every hump on the ground expecting to flush a bear.

They're at their smartest before they hole up, circling around for miles to throw you off, shoving a batch of dry grass into the den ahead of them, then using it to stuff the opening shut.

But the Natives have hunted autumn bears for generations, mostly with axes to save ammunition, and they really know the business. A bunch of broken blueberry bushes would mean nothing to a cheechako; to a Native, though, it's a good sign that there's a bear nearby. The females like blueberry branches for their beds, and break off all they can find around the den. Deep tracks in the snow mean bears heavy with food and about to hole up for the winter. Even their droppings tell a story, if you know how to read it: when they turn shiny and dark you know there's a well-fed bear around, ready to call it a season.

All these things, and more, my Uncle Johnny taught me, and it was a rare fall that I didn't pack home plenty of bear meat. But the one thing no one can teach you is common sense, so you're bound to make some foolish mistakes. And that's when you need plenty of luck because any mistake in this country can be the last one. Once, on an October morning when I wasn't even looking for bears, I came across some signs and tracked them to what looked like a really big den. But even after I'd shoveled the snow clear all around it, I couldn't tell where the hole was. I began poking around with the stock of my rifle and soon hit the soft spot. The rifle went clear through, but still I couldn't feel any bear in there, the way you were supposed to.

That's when I made my first mistake. I pulled the grass and stuff out of the hole and, lying stretched out on my stomach, I shoved the rifle as far in as I could, and when I still felt nothing, I shoved my arm all the way in, too. Then I felt a bear, all right—a ruffled and cranky bear who growled once, then slammed a paw down on the rifle and jerked it right out of my hand. I yanked my arm out of there as if I'd touched fire. The hair on the back of my neck stood on end as I realized what would have happened if that bear had grabbed a little farther up: he'd have laid my arm bare, or maybe even hauled me into the den for a midnight snack.

I sat down on my snowshoe to have a smoke and think the whole thing over. At that point, I was feeling a little shaky and, if it wasn't for the rifle, I'd have been satisfied to take off and forget the whole thing. But a man doesn't just leave a good .30-.30 behind. I figured that at least I ought to make an attempt to get it back. I kept remembering how Uncle Johnny went after bear with his ax, and wondered if I dared try that. Finally I decided I'd take a chance and unslung my ax. That was my second mistake.

First I cut some lengths of willow branch and plugged up the hole so that bear wouldn't come out and surprise me while I was busy working. Then I climbed up on top of the den and began chopping out an opening, the way I'd seen Uncle Johnny do, about a foot square. That would give me enough room for a good swing at the bear's head, but it was still small enough to slow him down if he suddenly decided to pop up that way. Pretty soon I could make out the steam from his breath and what looked like his head, and that's when I made my only smart move of the day. I went back to where I'd tied the dogs and turned them loose just in case.

They ran yelping up to the den, all excited by the bear smell, and I had to chase them off a little. Then I climbed on top, hefted the ax and swung down with all the strength I had.

All hell broke loose. I'd hit the bear, all right, but not cleanly. With a roar that shook the whole den, he came bursting up through that hole, spewing blood and dirt and moss in every direction. The narrow opening hadn't slowed him at all. He was clear to the hips and coming after me before I recovered enough balance to swing at him again. This time I took half his face off, but he kept coming, blinded and bellowing and swinging those massive paws at the torment he couldn't see.

The dogs had gone crazy. They were howling and tearing around, and as I watched for another shot at the bear I hollered at them to come help me, using language a man uses only on dogs. Then I saw that they were plenty busy: another bear had bulled through my willow sticks as though they weren't there and swung up on his hind legs, full of fight. He caught one dog and flung it fifteen feet through the air. The other three raced around trying to jump up on his back. But he was as quick as they were, and stronger, and shed them as if they were a swarm of gnats. Then a third bear came snarling into the open.

Man, was I in trouble! I thought about making a run for it, but the snow was so deep they'd have been on me before I went twenty feet. Besides, my dogs were taking a beating and there was still that damned rifle.

The first bear reached out for me and came down on the side of the den on all fours. I didn't miss that chance: I drove the ax down through his backbone, and though he lived for a little while, he couldn't make a move.

I guess I went half-crazy myself. I charged the closest bear, the one that had just come out. He stood looming over me, big claws all set to tear me open. Now there was no time to wait for a good opening. I crouched, then jumped straight up, bringing the ax up into his stomach with all my might, splitting it so the guts spilled into the snow, all bloody and hot. He screamed and slashed down and I felt those claws tear through my parka and the back of my arm. I swung up again, aiming lower this time, and the bear toppled forward, clutching himself and dying.

Three of the dogs were still worrying the third bear. He'd laid open the back of one dog and it lay whining and helpless under those tromping hind paws. I shrieked at the bear, full of anger and fear, and I swung at him as hard as I could. But now the ax had grown heavy in my hands, and my wild feelings spoiled my judgment. Instead of swinging up, I tried to come down on the bear from above, and all I did was cut his nose. He snatched the ax out of my hand and threw it away.

I dove for the den entrance. I felt claws raking my boots in the last instant before I scrambled in. I smelled the breath of him as he started in after me, blocking out the light and pinning me in there. I fumbled blindly on the ground, found my rifle and squirmed around to face him. That bear wasn't more than a foot away when I squeezed the trigger and blew his brains out.

I put my feet on his shoulder and shoved him back far enough so I could squeeze up out of the hole in the top of the den. For a second everything looked dazzling bright in the sun. Then I saw my mangled dog and felt the burning pain in my arm and I began to shake so hard that I couldn't even roll a smoke. I was panting for breath and covered with blood, and so was the snow for yards around. The first bear was still alive, so I went over and shot him in the head. Then I got some water for the hurt dog, but he couldn't drink it, not even when I held the cup. The flesh on his back was laid open to the bone and he was in agony. The others sniffed around him sadly, as if they knew he was finished. I got the rifle and ended the poor thing's suffering.

Still shaking, I bandaged my arm and brewed myself a pot of tea. I felt terrible about the dog—he had been a good worker and a good friend. I tried to concentrate on a Native saying of my Uncle Johnny's: "Don't cry when dogs die because dogs die and are born all the time; cry when a man dies because a man never comes back." I told myself that now I had meat for the winter and ribs for the next potlatch. But nothing much cheered me up.

It got so that I really looked forward to coming out of the bush for the summer. The people in the river villages—Hughes, Cutoff, Koyukuk Station, Nulato—all knew me by now and made me feel welcome. Even at Christmastime, if I wasn't catching too much fur, I'd hook up the dogs and ride overland to Hughes or Cutoff. They always had a big New Year's potlatch there: people who had got a bear would bring the ribs and backbone, and that sure made a nice feed. Then they'd dance all night.

There was always home brew—white mule—in a big barrel, the same one it had fermented in. The men would hang around telling stories and dipping their cups into it.

The longer they drank, the more stories you could hear going at the same time. Pretty soon the fights would start. Then those of us who weren't drinking, mostly the younger fellows, would have to separate the fighters and take them home. Some of them had to be taken home three or four times. There were always one or two who just wouldn't stay put, and finally we'd throw up our hands and let them fight it out. These usually wound up getting carried home. Next day they'd all get together again, headaches, bruises, and all, and shake hands as though they hadn't seen each other all winter. "Boy," they'd say, "we sure had a good time last night."

Some of the men played poker from dark to daybreak— that was their way of celebrating potlatch. You never saw a dollar of cash, but some real money changed hands. They would buy chips with their furs at the going price—so much for a muskrat, so much for a mink—and the way they tossed those skins into the pot you'd never guess at the sweat and struggle that went into the trapping. I've seen men lose a season's catch in one night, and then beg for credit so they could play some more.

Not that I was immune to temptation. I've lost my share of skins at poker, mostly because I never learned to quit trying to fill inside straights and three-card flushes. And I had my battle with white mule, too.

It happened the year I was seventeen, during a New Year's potlatch in Cutoff. It started out like the others, just fine, with the boys my age having fun leading the drunks home and joking about how foolish the men looked trying to fight when they could barely stand. Then, while we were lifting one of them into his cabin, a bottle of white mule fell out of his parka. I was going to set it inside the door, but Peter Weaselheart said, "He doesn't need that. He's had plenty."

We took it out in back of the store, and the boys passed it around and each one took a real swig. "Man, that's good stuff," Peter said, passing me the bottle. He didn't look as though it was good stuff. He looked as though he had swallowed beaver bile. But it suddenly dawned on me that this was not the first time these boys had swiped a bottle of mule, and I wasn't about to act like a cheechako. I tipped the bottle up and let it gurgle.

I'll never forget that first swallow. It was like wet fire, and it burned every inch of the way down to my stomach. Then it burned there. I forced myself not to gag, and it was quite a struggle.

"How is it?" someone said.

"Man," I told them, "that's good stuff."

They all laughed. "You're crazy," Peter Weaselheart said. "It's lousy. But it's free." I laughed with them. Then we finished the bottle and went looking for more.

It wasn't hard to find. By this time most of the men were pretty far gone and it was no trick to slip their bottles away from them. Before long, we were pretty far gone, too, and I was the worst of the lot. Maybe I was letting off steam after all my months alone in the bush. Maybe I was just trying to show everybody how tough Jimmy Huntington was. Whatever the reason, I soon got myself drunker than anyone else and was making more noise than all of them put together.

A woman came out of one of the houses and tried to get us to hush up and I shoved her down in the snow. Someone sent for my Uncle Johnny, and when he came running up to me I threw his hand off my arm and squared away to fight him. I had spent plenty of time watching the men in action when they got drunk and I guess I figured that this was the way it was done. "C'mon," I kept mumbling to Uncle Johnny, "put 'em up. I'll fight anybody." He just looked at me as though I were a stranger, and finally he turned away sadly and went home.

After a while I went behind a snowbank and was sick. That cleared my head a little and I realized that most of the boys, who had their hands full with me, had given up in disgust and gone home. The few who were left were too stupefied to come in out of the cold. I dragged myself back to my uncle's house and stumbled around in the kitchen trying to get my bedroll fixed. He came out of the bedroom and lit the coal-oil lamp.

I didn't want to look at him. "I'm sorry I woke you up," I said, trying to crawl into the bedroll with my boots on.

"Boy, I haven't been to sleep yet," he said. "Here, drink this." He was reaching a cup of hot coffee down to me.

"I'm too sick to drink it." I wanted to die.

"Drink it!"

He was in charge again and somehow that made me feel better. I took the coffee and the strong hot smell of it wasn't too bad. I took a little sip.

Uncle Johnny sat down on a box near the bedroll. "What were you trying to do," he said, "show those boys that you're all Indian?"

I looked up at him. I didn't know what he was talking about.

"You're a half-breed, understand, and no matter how tough you act or how drunk you get you'll still be a half-breed. But you have nothing to be ashamed of. Your mother was a strong, brave woman, and your father was the best white man I ever knew. All these people liked him. They like you. You don't have to prove anything to them. Understand?"

I nodded. I did understand, finally. And Uncle Johnny

was right: I guess I had been a little mixed up about what I was, who I was. That's why I had to stay out in the bush longer than anyone else and bring in the most skins—and drink the most white mule.

"You're a good boy," Uncle Johnny was saying. "You'll learn, otherwise I wouldn't waste my time telling you all this. Now go to sleep."

Next day was the worst time of all. Besides the miserable sick feeling in my stomach and head, I had to find the woman I'd thrown down and tell her I was sorry. I sure didn't want to, but my uncle said that if a man didn't face the truth he'd have to hide from it for the rest of his life. The woman was very nice. She said it was all right, that I was drunk and didn't know what I was doing.

"No," I told her, "I knew everything I was doing, but I'll never do it again."

For ten years after that night, I didn't have a drink of any kind. Then I began to take an occasional beer. And to this day, that's it. In the beginning, the hardest part was that other people kept trying to force whiskey on me. Either they thought I was kidding or they weren't happy unless everybody was drunk, like them. But I just kept saying no, and after a while they quit trying.

I still had some hard knocks ahead of me: just learning to be among people was always harder for me than getting along in the wilderness. As soon as I reached town, it seemed, I'd do something silly. And the older I got the more I kept wanting to live off the store shelf. Why pick blueberries when you could buy plenty of canned fruit, or make snowshoes when Pop Russell would sell you a good pair—on credit? All of a sudden paddling got to be too much work, and I went broke buying gasoline.

I could think of more ways to waste money! Early one spring, before the ice was even out of the river, I decided to take my team down to Nulato and sell the few skins I had. Not long after I reached Cutoff, an airplane landed on the river. There was a fur buyer aboard and he offered to take my catch on the spot. I was sure tempted— the boys were all coaxing me to stay around and have some fun—but I owed Pop Russell from the year before and had to say no. Then the pilot spoke up: he said he'd carry me to Nulato and back for ninety dollars. That seemed like a fine idea, so I loaded my skins aboard and the people lined the riverbank to watch us take off with a whoosh and a roar.

That old junker wouldn't be allowed in the air today. One of the wing struts was made of nothing but plain baling wire, the ski had a broken shock cord, and the wind came whipping through the cabin as though we were sitting in the open. But we made it to Nulato and back, a hundred and ninety miles, in four hours. That was sure traveling for those days: the best I could have done with the dogs was a week. I really enjoyed that trip.

There was only one thing wrong. By the time I settled up with Pop Russell and paid the pilot, I had exactly fifteen dollars coming for my catch—which meant that I'd have to buy my new grubstake on credit again.

When I got back to Cutoff, broke, as usual, one of the older men asked me if I'd help him run off the barrel of mash he had working in a corner of his cabin. I said sure, so he dug out some coil and a couple of old gasoline cans and we went to work, heating the mash on the Yukon stove, running it through another can that we cooled by packing it in snow, and burning off the drippings. It took us nearly all night to cool that barrel, but when we were finished, we had twelve catsup bottles and two jars full of white mule. The old man swallowed a good-sized sample, shuddered, and said, "Son, that's just right!" Sure, I thought, looking at his sour face and puckered-up mouth, I bet it is.

When we hauled the stuff into town, that old boy was welcomed as though he'd just come back from two years in the Native hospital at Anchorage. Men ran up to shake his hand and slap his back, and everybody was his best friend. I noticed that nobody went out of their way to shake my hand. Before the old man had even got his dogs unhooked, he'd sold eleven catsup bottles, collecting five muskrat skins for each. Figuring a dollar a skin, you can see that a lot of trapping went into that whiskey. The only reason the old man finally closed up shop was that he was never one to hang back himself when it came to belting down mule. "The trouble with me," he said, "is that I got too many friends."

He offered me a bottle for my trouble, but I had no use for it. Instead, I asked him if he would give me some tips on home brewing and lend me his mash barrel for a while. It had hit me in a big, bright flash that when it came to making money, brewing mash had it all over chasing mink and marten. The old man said sure, and for as long as he stayed sober, I got a fine education in the art of home brew. By next morning, I'd picked up twenty-five catsup bottles around town, loaded the barrel on my sled, and was on my way back to Hogatza to begin my career as a bootlegger.

When I got back to my camp, I set the barrel up on two gas cans and dumped twenty-five pounds of sugar, ten pounds of cornmeal and two yeast cakes into it. I put a lantern under it to keep it warm. Then I brewed some tea and sat down to watch it.

On the third day it finally began to work and I tore myself away long enough to start building the still. Ten days later it was still bubbling and I'd run out of meat so I had to leave it to do some hunting. On the fifteenth day it looked ready. All the time I was running it off my brain was clicking out figures—if I got three gallons, I could fill the twenty-five catsup bottles and all the jars I'd found around the cabin, and at five rat skins a bottle . . .

Man, I'd be rich!

In my enthusiasm, I put up another barrel. It was half finished before I realized that I didn't have so much as a tin can to put the brew in. I fiddled around trying to make a small barrel, but it didn't hold water any better than a fishnet. Finally an idea came to me. I went out to the woods and cut down a birch about eight inches thick. Then I sawed off a two-foot length and took it back to the cabin. Augering, chiseling and carving, I got the thing hollowed out, made a plug for the end and let the whole works sit in water for a couple of days so it wouldn't soak up any mule. Now I had a homemade keg to carry three more gallons. That would fill thirty or more catsup bottles, and at five dollars a bottle . . .

By now the ice was out of the river. I loaded the Ark and headed downstream for Cutoff at full tilt, counting money in my head all the way. It didn't take long for the word to spread that Jimmy Huntington was in town with white mule for sale, and now I was everybody's long-lost friend. In something less than an hour, I'd got rid of all twenty-five catsup bottles and two of the jars. In exchange, I had a fine pile of muskrats, nearly a hundred and fifty of them, all skinned and dried.

I had planned to stay over and sell the mule in my keg to these same men, but they got so drunk on the first batch that I figured it would be a week before they were in shape to start drinking again. Besides, I didn't think there were that many more skins left in town. So I decided that in the morning I'd go down to the mouth of the Kateel River. There were always lots of hunters camped there, and I'd have no trouble trading off the rest of my brew. I bedded down for the night but couldn't fall asleep for a long time because of the racket. I lay on the deck of the Ark listening to those men cursing and carousing, and thinking how foolish they were. Every now and then you'd hear the scared voice of a woman, begging her man to come home.

Just after daybreak, when the drunks were sleeping it off, I went around town and picked up all the empty catsup bottles. Riding down to the Kateel, I refilled them from the keg and was ready for business when I pulled into the hunters' camp. They were glad to see me, too, although they tried to buy my mule for three skins a bottle. There was no argument. I had the mule and they had the muskrats and they went and got them, five skins a bottle.

They had a big tent pitched on the bank. A bunch of them were playing poker there, and they asked me if I wanted to take a hand. I thought: pretty soon they'll be blind drunk and won't be able to tell an ace from a deuce, and I'll walk out of that camp with everything but their mukluks. "Sure," I said, and threw fifty skins into the bank for chips.

But a funny thing happened. Those hunters were too smart to get drunk. They worked on three bottles of mule, and that's all. They were saving the rest for a celebration when they got back to their villages, they said. And they had plenty to celebrate, because they were also too smart to draw to inside straights and three-card flushes, and they cleaned me barer than a bear's belly in spring. In three hours I was stone broke, without a muskrat skin to my name. Not one.

Sick at heart and disgusted with myself, I started back upriver. By the time I got to Cutoff I was tired and really wanted to stop, but I was too ashamed. I kept on going, all the way back to Hogatza, thinking, I'm sure, to get that barrel working again and brew up another batch of mule right away, at least enough to pay for an outfit for the winter. But I kept thinking of the foolishness and fighting that came out of that barrel, and I kept hearing those women in Cutoff calling their men home, and I began to wonder if maybe losing everything was all a man could expect when he made everything on other men's weakness in the first place. So I took the still outside and smashed it to little pieces with the ax, and that was the end of my short career as a bootlegger.

In 1936, in the spring of the year, I met a girl I liked well enough to marry. Her name was Cecelia Olin, and her people fished in a camp near the mouth of the Huslia River. According to the Native ways, we were both pretty old to be still single—I was nearly twenty and Cecelia was past sixteen and her father invited me to move in with them on the spot. I told him I appreciated the offer but would rather wait another year: that would give me one more trapping season to accumulate some money, so I wouldn't have to come to my new wife dead broke. Also maybe I could arrange for the minister to ride upriver and marry us in the right way.

But as it happened, that next winter turned out to be

the worst for fur I could ever remember. There was practically no mink, and my entire catch consisted of about seventy-five muskrats, which were as many skins as anybody else brought in, either. Furthermore, I never did make contact with the minister, so when I came out of the bush in the spring things weren't any different for Cecelia and me than they'd been the year before. But now she said she did not want to wait anymore, that if we had no money she would eat fish, the same as I did, and that's the way it was. Her father gave us a big potlatch and everybody shook my hand and Cecelia said, "Well, I guess we're married." And when we woke up in the morning we were.

We planned to go down to the old fishing camp below Nulato. At least my seventy-five skins would pay for a summer outfit, which was a lucky thing: old Pop Russell had died that winter, and people said the new trader wasn't so good-natured about credit. We hung around Nulato for a few days. Cecelia wanted to get started, but I had a certain feeling and told her to take it easy. And sure enough, the minister came down the river one fine morning and I rushed off to buy a fifty-cent wedding ring and had him marry us properly. Then I felt better.

We were happy in the fishing camp. The salmon were running as thick as always, and whenever we were in real need of groceries or anything, I could bundle up six or eight bales of dried fish and take them to Nulato to trade. It was on one of those trips that I heard how the Territory was hiring men to start work on an airfield just outside the town. I thought about that for a long time. I had never worked for wages, and I didn't much like the idea of it: a man ought to have only one boss, himself. But summer doesn't last forever. Unless I could put together enough money to buy a trapping outfit, we faced some tough times. Besides, Cecelia was going to have a baby.

One evening, an old Native and his wife came paddling up the river. We hollered for them to stop, and Cecelia made tea and some nice duck stew for them. The man began to talk about the old days in Alaska, and it reminded me of the stories Dad used to tell. I could have sat there listening to him all night. Then he said that times were changing, that people weren't satisfied any more to stay in camp and hunt and fish and eat what the land provided. "The young people all want to hang around the towns now," he said. "They want to eat the white man's food and drink mule." He patted my arm. "It's good to see a couple that still knows how to live off the land. That's the best life."

I didn't know what to say. I felt a little guilty because I surely wasn't all the old Native believed I was. Anyway, I think I was beginning to see that times were changing even more than he imagined. The people had had a taste of store food and they liked it, and was that really so bad? They wanted electric lights and radios and gas kickers for their boats, too, and the young ones would never be satisfied any more to shoot a bear and live alone all winter eating off his ribs. And in the morning, when the old Native and his missus went paddling up the river, I told Cecelia that I was going to take that job at the airport.

It wasn't too bad. I started out swinging a pick, like all the others, but one day the oiler broke down and I poked around and finally fixed it. The boss was so happy he said I could be the driver of it. I went riding up and down the strip, dumping oil on the stretches they'd cleared and flattened. For this they paid me seven dollars a day, seven days a week, so you can see the money really piled up.

Cecelia liked it, too. We had moved into town and she made some nice friends. She sure wasn't happy when it got to be September and I told her to start packing for the trip back up the Koyukuk. "They'll be working on the field until snow falls," she said. "Why do you have to quit now?"

I didn't know exactly what to tell her. That since I'd been twelve the first hint of autumn had always turned me north? That trapping was still all I knew and that I had to be ready to trap when the season opened?

"I've got enough money for my grubstake," I finally said. "I have to be back up at Hogatza before freeze-up.

She stomped around for a while, but there was nothing else I could think of to say that might cheer her up. Maybe next year would be different, but I didn't know that for sure, and meanwhile it was this year and I had to go.

We got to Cutoff in the middle of the month, and I left Cecelia with her parents. I said I would try to make it back before the baby was born, but I could tell that she wasn't counting on it. Only my father-in-law understood: "You will lose a good week's trapping if you come down in December. Besides, what can you do for her? She has her mother."

I was glad to have that advice because, as it turned out, there was plenty of fur that year, and I didn't want to leave my traps. It was March before I got back, and by then my baby daughter was two months old. They had named her Christine, and when Cecelia put her in my arms I was afraid to breathe, she was that tiny. Then I didn't want to let her go.

After a while Cecelia said, "You told me you'd come down before she was born."

"We're a family now. We need money," I said. "I figured it was more important to build up a stake for us than to waste a lot of time mushing back and forth visiting."

She nodded. I think she understood.

In June, we went a hundred and fifty miles up the Hogatza to the mouth of Caribou Creek. I had heard about some abandoned gold diggings that were open for new staking, and since there was supposed to be a heavy salmon run up that way, it seemed as good a place as any to make a summer camp. Now I was really looking to put together some cash. I loved the trapping life but it was beginning to look as though it was over for me—how could a man go off and leave his wife and daughter every winter? And so my father's old dream of running a little trading post somewhere slowly took hold of me. All I thought about was getting enough money to start.

I spent long hours putting up drying racks and emptying the fish wheel. One day, when the smokehouse was almost finished, we heard a gas boat coming up from downstream, and I sent Cecelia to put up some tea. It was the bishop of the Episcopal Church making his annual trip to the camps and villages along the river. We were sure glad to see him, for now the baby could be baptized. Afterward, he gave Cecelia and me Holy Communion, and we had a nice tea. Then he was off again on his long, lonely trip.

We ate well that summer. There was plenty of bear around the camp, and since fresh meat doesn't keep more than a few days in the July heat, there was no sense in saving any. We ate the best of the salmon, and one day I shot a couple of geese, and Cecelia made a good stew. It was fine living—except for the mosquitoes. We had to keep a net over Christine.

When the salmon run was past its peak, I walked back out to the creeks. Gold colors showed almost every place I panned, but I was a long way from getting excited. I knew enough from listening to Dad to realize that a man working alone couldn't take enough out of these creeks even to pay for his labor. The only chance to make a dollar was to get some big mining outfit interested and sell out. I strolled around, taking plenty of time, and staked the eight claims I was allowed, four for me, four for Cecelia. When I got back to camp, I wrote a letter to the Commissioner in Fairbanks telling about my claims, then got in the boat and went forty miles downstream to the mouth of the Hogatza where the mail boat went by once a month or so. I stuck a pole into the bank, hung a gasoline can on it and put the letter inside. I sure hoped they noticed it.

A couple of Eskimos came up the river in a canoe one August afternoon and we made a lunch for them. Things had changed a lot between the Eskimos and Indians since my mother's day. We didn't exactly consider ourselves blood brothers, but at least we didn't shoot each other on sight. These two, a boy of fifteen or so and an older man named Henry, were on their way home to Kobuk, where the Pah River bends north of the Arctic Circle, and they still had a long portage to make. I asked them what they were doing in Indian country, and they said they'd come down to see how the hunting was.

That ticked me off. I know it's a free country, but I didn't like the idea of somebody scouting the game and then bringing back a whole pack of Eskimo hunters. But what really got me mad was the older one's bragging about what a good shot he was with that Luger pistol tucked in his pants. "I killed a bear with it yesterday," he said. "One shot."

I asked him where the meat was. I didn't see it in the canoe. He shrugged. "We left it. No sense packing meat when there's so much around."

I just looked at him. I think the younger one knew what was on my mind because he got nervous and edged away from the fire. Finally I said, "The game in this country was put here to feed the people—the Indians. We don't kill it just to prove what good shots we are, and nobody else is going to kill it for no reason, either." I stood up and he scrambled back, as if he thought I was going to hit him. "This party's over, Mister. You can make your camp down on the beach, but you better be way upriver when I wake up tomorrow."

Cecelia was afraid he'd try to hurt us during the night, but I knew better. I'd seen men like that before—Eskimos, Indians, and white men—the kind that do everything with their mouths. When you make them shut up they're finished. I felt sorry for the boy, though.

In the morning they were gone. But we weren't done with them yet, not quite. In that hour of the evening when the mosquitoes are still, Cecelia and I were sitting on the bank smoking and watching the last of the salmon struggle up the river. Suddenly I felt her stiffen beside me and when I looked upstream I saw why: the Eskimos' canoe had just come around the bend, and the boy was paddling hard toward our camp. There was no sign of the other one.

I got up and started for the beach. Cecelia tried to catch me. "Take your rifle," she said.

"I don't need any rifle. They're in trouble."

They sure were. Henry, the older one, lay in the bottom of the canoe more dead than alive, his clothes all torn, and his body, too, what you could see of it. Most of him was caked with dried blood. The boy's face was white as snow, but he kept his voice steady when he asked if I would help them. "He went into the woods after a wounded bear," he said.

He didn't have to tell me that. There is a certain look to a man, or what's left of him, when a bear gets through mauling him. This was it. "Let's pack him up to the bank," I said.

He groaned when we fetched him out from the bottom of the canoe. He tried to talk, but it was hopeless: his mouth was torn open from the left corner to the socket of his left eye, and his tongue just flopped around in that big, bloody opening. Cecelia took one look, then shuddered and turned away. I told her to boil up some hot water.

We laid him on a piece of canvas and I cut his clothes off to see if there was any sense in prolonging his agony. Sometimes the kindest thing you can do for a man who's tangled with a bear is to speed him on his way. I had a hunch that maybe that was what the Eskimo was trying to ask me for when I lifted him out of the canoe.

His right arm was laid open from the shoulder to the wrist. His right thigh was torn, too, and full of holes where the bear had bitten him. There were deep claw marks at the back of his neck. Then the bear had really dug in and all but torn the scalp from his head. It looked as though he had a couple of broken ribs, too, but that would have to wait.

When the hot water was ready, I stirred a cup of table salt into it and began washing the wounds. That's all we had by way of medicine, but I figured it didn't much matter: if God weren't with this man, all the medicine in Fairbanks wouldn't help him. When I'd cleaned him as well as I could, I poured more salt into the deeper wounds. He moaned, but that wasn't the half of it. I had to stuff it into those holes in his thigh, and my fingers went all the way in, and he screamed and passed out. That was the best thing for him since I hadn't even started to sew up his face.

I was going to use caribou sinew, but when I went to get some Cecelia told me it would rot in his skin and come apart. She said to use the hair from his head and she gave me a bone needle that she used for sewing moccasins. But she didn't come out of the tent.

I pulled a bunch of hairs out of his head, taking care not to rip the rest of his scalp off. His hair was just right, nice and thick, and I threw it into the boiling salt water, along with the needle. Then I took a good long look at his face and the top of his head, trying to figure out the best way to sew him together. All this time the boy hadn't said a word, only watching and helping me whenever he could. But as soon as I pulled those two flaps of mouth together and stuck the needle through, I lost my helper for good. He clapped a hand over his mouth and ran for the bushes, and I could hear him being mighty sick.

I sewed away until the sun was low on the horizon, and I couldn't see too well anymore. Then I called for Cecelia to bring the coal-oil lamp. She wasn't happy about it, but she stuck right with me, even when she had to hold the lamp close enough so I could see to take the last few stitches inside his mouth. Altogether it had taken nearly four hours. Henry wouldn't be any beauty—if he lived— but I had done the best for him that I knew how.

I got the boy to help me fix his bedroll on the ground and lift him in. We put a mosquito net over him, and sat there for a little while listening to him struggle for breath. The boy asked me if I thought he was going to die. I said I didn't know, but that there wasn't anything more we could do about it, either way.

"I'm sorry I ran away," the boy said.

"Forget it. Next time you won't." I asked him how it had all happened.

They had come on the bear about twelve miles up the river, he said, a big blackie slapping salmon up on the beach. Before the boy could stop him, Henry had that Luger out and shot the bear in the side. The bear went roaring into the woods, and Henry went in right after him, not even waiting until the bear had stiffened up some so it couldn't move so fast. The boy had to tie up the canoe, then followed with a .22. He heard the bear charge and Henry screaming, and he'd run toward them, firing the rifle in the air and yelling as loud as he could. It worked. When he reached the place where his partner lay, the bear was gone, scared away. But the damage had been done. Henry was ripped and mangled as only a bear can do it, and the boy dragged him back to the canoe and made for the nearest help, our camp.

"Even among my people he is known as a big mouth," the boy said now, looking at the ground. "But he is one of my people. I thank you for him."

"Let's wait to see if there's anything to thank me for," I told him. "Anyway, there's one good thing: I don't think he'll be coming down this way to hunt anymore."

Very early in the morning the boy shook me awake. "I think he is dying now," he said.

I went out to have a look. Henry's breath was coming in noisy little rasps. He seemed to be choking and was burning up with fever. I put my arm under his shoulders and raised him as much as I dared. Then I sent the boy for some water, and managed to get a couple of spoonfuls into him. Once he'd swallowed whatever was backed up in his throat he breathed a little easier.

I made the boy some breakfast. His eyes were dark with strain and exhaustion, and I guessed he'd stayed up all night, watching his friend. He wanted to know if I thought it would be better to put Henry in the boat and take him down to the Yukon, maybe to the hospital at Tanana.

"That's a three-week trip," I said, "and he wouldn't last three days on the river. His only chance is to stay right where he is."

We built a lean-to over him to keep the sun off. The boy squatted right by his side, hour after hour, wiping the sweat from his face and shooing the mosquitoes off. On the third day the fever broke and Henry opened his eyes. "My chest hurts," he said.

I was surprised that he could talk. His face was so swollen that you couldn't tell where his mouth ended and his eye began. I tore some strips of canvas and bound up the broken ribs. Then he wanted to see himself in a looking glass. I told him he looked better than before but that he'd have to wait until I took the stitches out to see. Cecelia cooked up a fish broth and fed it to him, and he seemed to enjoy it.

On the fourth day we helped him get to his feet so he wouldn't stiffen up. He could move pretty well with only a little support. Next day I pulled the stitches out and gave him the looking glass. He didn't look so bad: the scar was nice and straight, except that I didn't get the corner of his mouth quite right so that he seemed to be forever grinning at something. But he was satisfied.

"Where'd you learn about sewing up a person?" he asked.

"By working on you," I said. "The hard way. Same as you learned about hunting bear."

He had nothing to say to that.

In another ten days he felt strong enough to travel. Of course he was in no shape to make that portage over to the Pah, so I told them to go downriver and have the doctor at Tanana make sure I hadn't done anything wrong. When they left, Henry shook my hand and said, "If you're ever in my country, I'll try to thank you the right way."

At the end of August Cecelia and I went back to Cutoff. There was no letter waiting for me with good news about my claims so all I could do was go back up to the winter cabin at Hogatza and trap fur again. This time, though, Cecelia said that she and the baby were going with me. "It can't be any worse than staying alone," she told me.

We went by dogsled not long after freeze-up, Christine all wrapped in blankets and fur. It wasn't too bad: it never got much colder than twenty or thirty below, and there was a fair number of mink around. When the trapping tapered off we decided to go back to Cutoff for the Christmas potlatch, and to stock up on some supplies.

But there was bad news waiting for us at Cutoff. The store had burned down and, except for some fresh meat the men brought in, there was no food in the whole town— no flour for bread, no potatoes or canned vegetables and, worst of all, no milk for the babies. Nor would any come in until breakup, unless someone went and got it.

That night Cecelia and I talked it over. I remembered that the Eskimo boy had told me about a trading post not far from Kobuk. If I got some other men to go with me, we could take three or four dog teams up and bring back the things people needed. It was probably a hundred miles each way, but with good weather we could do that in a week. Meanwhile, Cecelia and the baby could stay with her parents.

There was no shortage of volunteers. None of us had ever been up in Eskimo country, and this seemed like a good opportunity to look it over: we had skins to trade, and since the one called Henry owed me his life, his people ought to be pretty nice to my people. Early next morning five of us driving four teams headed out. We didn't know the way so we just followed the Dakili River north, then crossed over the divide to the head of the Selawik. That was the end of the timber country. Up ahead the snow and the slow rolling hills stretched out to the sky. It seemed as though you could see forever, and there was nothing to see, only that endless white land. We were just about at the Arctic Circle now and figured it was fifty miles more to the Kobuk.

We camped under the last trees and cut enough firewood to carry for the trip. In the morning, when we'd been on the trail about three hours, we saw our first caribou. They were less than half a mile away, a good-sized herd of them, moving slowly across the hills in front of us. I led the teams into a hollow and told three of the men to keep the dogs quiet and out of sight. The other man and I grabbed our rifles and started trotting toward the herd, bent low to the ground so they wouldn't spot us. We didn't know the first thing about hunting caribou—you just don't see them in our part of the country—but we meant to give it a try because the people in Cutoff would need all the fresh meat they could get.

When we were still three hundred yards away, the herd turned in our direction. We hit the ground and, lying prone in the snow, lined them up in our sights. I thought: this is too good to be true. It was. Whether the dogs had caught the caribou smell or were excited by something else, I never did find out, but all at once you could hear them howling clear across the tundra. My partner and I each had time for one quick shot before the herd swerved to the west and took off like a brown blur on the snow.

We stood up to see if we'd had any luck when, suddenly, the howling was right on us and we spun around to see two teams of dogs flying by, sleds and all. They were hell-bent for those caribou—and the caribou were hell-bent straight down the Selawik Valley with not a tree or a rock or a bush to slow them down. I have never seen game travel so fast—and the dogs were gaining on them!

Our troubles had only begun. Down in the hollow, we could hear the other men fighting to hold the rest of the dogs in, and we ran for all we were worth to give them a hand. We had already lost two teams, and if the other two got loose in this godforsaken land we'd really be in for it. I dived for the nearest sled and dug my heels into the snow to brake it. But those dogs had gone absolutely crazy.

They yowled and pulled for all they were worth, and the towline broke and away they went and all I had hold of was the sled. I jumped to my feet—too late. The last team had just broken away from the three men hanging onto it. We now had forty-six dogs running wild across the open tundra.

For a while we just stood there, five dummies trying to work up the ambition to take out after our teams on foot. Then the dark specks strung out along the white valley seemed to grow darker, bigger. The caribou had begun a cautious swing to the left.

"We must have dropped their leader," I said. "They're coming back."

We came running up out of the hollow and, from the next hill, saw the dead caribou: one of the two shots we'd fired had made a lucky hit. When we got close enough we could see that it was the leader. He had a tremendous rack of antlers and the scuffed, hairless neck of a fighter. The rest of the herd was a mile away, the dogs maybe four hundred yards behind them, and they were still coming on.

I sent the other men to hide behind the crest of the hill and I dropped down behind the dead animal. I made myself hold fire until the herd was less than fifty feet away. Then I opened up, squeezing off shots until my rifle was empty. Back up on the hill, I could hear the others pumping away just as hard, and I saw three, maybe four caribou drop. But it was like trying to turn back a blizzard with a fly swatter. By the time the leaders veered off, the rest of them were all over me—and those crazy, yapping dogs came swarming right up their backs.

The other men, unable to shoot anymore for fear of hitting me, were running off the hill with their knives out.

I never had a chance to go for mine. All I could see was flashing caribou hooves and I burrowed in under the dead one trying to protect myself.

Then the dogs hit—forty-six raving, rattle-brained malamutes, tangled in their tow lines and fighting and biting anything they could sink their teeth into. One of them even went to work on my leg and that was his big mistake of the day. I clouted him on the head with my rifle stock and jumped to my feet, just as wrought up as the dogs were now, swinging at every one I could reach. Pretty soon I had half of them laid out, and all the fight had gone out of the others. The caribou were gone and I stood there in the sudden deathly quiet, breathing so hard it hurt and feeling the sweat soaking my underclothes. All around, where the men had fought the caribou with their knives, the snow was splattered with blood. We had killed six of them. The dogs were flung over a fifty-foot area, but they weren't going anyplace, not even the ones who were still conscious. They had their lines so hopelessly snarled that it would take us an hour just to separate the teams.

My legs turned all rubbery and I sank down in the snow. Man, I thought, we were a great pack of hunters! Losing our dogs! Fighting caribou with knives! I made up my mind to warn the others that we'd better just keep this whole mess our little secret—as soon as I could talk again.

One of them had made a fire and brought me some melted snow to drink. That was a big help. "I was on my way over to give you a hand with the dogs," he said. "But the way you were swinging that rifle around I figured I better stay put."

That reminded me of my leg. I hiked my pants up to have a look and found three neat little holes where teeth had gone through. I stuffed some table salt in them and tied the leg with a strip of flour sack, and it hardly bothered me at all.

I sat there coaxing my strength back while the other boys untangled the dogs. They were sure quiet now, pretending to be friendly as pups. After the lacing I'd given them they'd have jumped a foot if anybody said, "Boo!" Once they were straightened out, all of us went to work skinning out the caribou. We cached the meat and marked it for the return trip, then had some tea and a lunch and set off again.

We had to make only one more camp. By that first afternoon, we'd come on an old dog-team trail and followed it straight to the river. Next day we were in Kobuk.

The people seemed friendly enough. They poured out of every house and alleyway and swarmed around us, jabbering and gaping as though we'd come from another world. In a way, I suppose, you could say that we did. One thing for sure: this place and its people, the first Eskimo town we had ever been in, was as strange to us as we were to them. Everything was different. You didn't see a single thing made of wood. The houses looked just like the round igloos you see in picture books. Later I found out they were actually built up with squares of sod, and that snow blocks were laid on for extra protection. Even their dogs were hitched in a different way.

Suddenly, in that great babbling mob, I heard someone call, "Jim Huntington!" It was the boy who had been in our fishing camp the summer before, looking twice as big in his parka and wolverine ruff, grinning as he elbowed through the crowd and pumped my hand. "What are you doing up in this country?"

I told him we were after supplies, and he said the trading post was only eight miles up the river and would have everything we needed. Then he said, "Now you come to my house and eat a meal." I tried to explain that I had to take care of my dogs, and that there were four other men with me. But it seems as though you don't tell the Eskimo anything when you're in his country: you just do what he says. The boy said something to his people in their language, and the next thing I knew our dogs were led away and each one of my friends was being escorted to a different igloo.

We had to bend real low to get into the boy's house, going through a long tunnel that came out in a fair-sized room lit with a seal-oil lamp and full of the people of his family, from little tots to a grandmother who must have been old when the Russians owned Alaska. Everybody kowtowed to her. The boy told them who I was and then we sat down to eat—dried salmon, muktuk, caribou meat, crackers, and a good strong tea. The old grandmother asked me how come I was so far from home. I told her about the store in Cutoff burning down. I said I came to buy shells and food and milk for my baby.

She rolled a cigarette and lit it, never taking her eyes off me. "What's the matter with your wife, no more milk?" she said. "How old him baby?"

"She is a girl baby. She is two years old."

"How long you and wife stay together?"

"Three years."

"Three years, only one baby come? Ha! Maybe you don't stay home enough. Maybe you work too much."

I told her I was out on the trap line most of the time.

She blew smoke in my face and said, "Maybe you stay home two moon. After that, ha, some more baby come. Then you don't have to buy milk in store."

I said I would give it a try. I figured I had to be polite to her. I even thanked her for the advice. But I was sure desperate to change the subject. I turned to the boy and asked, "How's your friend Henry? What did the doctor in Tanana say about my sewing job?"

The igloo got very quiet. I thought for sure I'd put my foot in it again. Finally the boy spoke: "The doctor said you did a good job. There was no more he could do."

I felt better. I said, "Well, where is the great bear hunter? I'd like to say hello."

The boy shook his head. "Right after the first frost he took a team out on the river. Nobody could tell him anything, that the ice was still thin. You know. He went in less than a mile from here—dogs, sled, and all. The only thing we ever found was the hole."

Man, that made me mad—after the way I'd worked to keep that man alive! But all I said was, "That's too bad."

The grandmother spoke up again: "He was looking for death. If not bear or ice, he find some other way to die. He a man who not meant to grow old."

I nodded. She was a smart old lady, after all.

Pretty soon some other people came and said that now I had to go eat in their house. Just to be nice I ate some more muktuk and drank some more tea. I had no more than finished when they took me to another house, and still another, and in each one there was a big feed. It got so that all I could manage to get down was the tea. I drank so much tea that I felt as though my back teeth were afloat. I asked them where the bathroom was, but they didn't seem to understand. I tried every word I knew —privy, restroom, toilet—but all I got was a blank look, so finally I told them in plain English what I needed.

They laughed and laughed. "Oh, anyplace outside," they said.

I went outside, but there were kids playing around everywhere so I kept going until I'd walked all the way to the river. And there were still people around. Pretty soon I came across two of my buddies with the same problem. "Say, where's a guy supposed to go in this place?" they asked.

I told them that the Eskimos had given us permission to use any part of the arctic land for that purpose, and I stood there as though I were admiring the view and did what I had to do; not one person even looked up. Later I discovered that the Eskimos always did the same. They weren't troubled by any two-faced modesty, and let's face it, in a land where there wasn't a bush or a bit of cover, that makes a lot of sense.

As I wandered along the riverbank looking for our dogs, a big, strong-looking man with a vaguely familiar face came up to me. He said that my bedroll and things had been taken to his house, that I was to spend the night there. In the morning, he would put me on the trail to the trading post. I told him that that was okay with me, it didn't make any difference where I stayed, but that I had to buy some dried fish for my dogs first.

"Dogs already eat," he said. "We take care."

I thanked him—that was really service! We walked by the dogs on the way to his house and I got the barest wag of their tails as I passed, that's how contented they were. His house was bigger than the others, and it had more people in it, including a whole flock of kids belonging to the unmarried daughters. The Eskimos saw nothing wrong with this. In fact, they told me later that a girl didn't have much chance of marrying until she'd proved she could have babies.

I saw my bedroll in the tunnel so I sat down on it to put my moose skin slippers on. No sooner had I pulled my mukluks off than one of the daughters, a nice-looking girl of seventeen or so, took them from me, brushed them clean, and hung them up. When I rolled a cigarette, she got me a saucer for an ashtray. I told her thanks, and she sat by my feet without looking at me. But I'll be darned if she wasn't blushing!

The man who brought me said, "Now you tell us about my son, how you sewed him up."

Then I understood: this was Henry's house, his family.

The man was his father—that was why he looked familiar and I was brought here last because theirs was to be the honor of having me spend the night with them. Little did I know what that was going to lead to.

I cleared my throat and told them the story of Henry and the bear, stretching it out and trying to make their son look less foolish than he had been, and as brave as possible. I was positive that they had heard the story before— Henry and the boy must have told them something about it. But they were pretending as hard as I was, oohing and aahing in all the right places and bending toward me as though they couldn't wait for the next words out of my mouth.

Meanwhile, more and more people came crawling through the tunnel into the igloo to hear the story. It was packed from wall to wall, and the heat was suffocating and the smell from the seal-oil lamp was enough to knock you out. Every once in a while the girl who had taken care of my mukluks bent over and mopped the sweat from my forehead with a towel. Finally the story was over and the father shooed all the visitors out. "Now we drink some tea and eat," he said, and I did my best not to look sick. While the women were putting the food on a canvas table, he drew me aside and said, "You were good to my son, and I give you my thanks." I tried to tell him that anyone would have tried to help but he shushed me: "It is not only that you saved his life. It is that you made him seem manly to our people. I was his father and I know that he was otherwise. But he is dead now. It is good that people think well of him." He took my hand and said, "Anything I have is yours."

It seemed as though that damned Henry was never going to quit making trouble for me!

I nibbled at the food, and the girl brought me tea. She put sugar in it. She asked me if I wanted anything else and I said no, I was fine. Pretty soon I realized that the old man had turned the lamp down and that everyone was going off to a different corner to sleep. I went out to the tunnel and took my slippers off—and there was the girl. She took the slippers and set them down beside my parka. I crawled into the bedroll and she blew the lamp out and crawled in with me.

I said, "Listen—what's your name?"

"Kitty."

"Yes. Well, listen, Kitty, don't you have a bed?"

"Yes, this."

"You mean you're going to sleep with me?"

"No, *you* sleep with *me*. This is *my* place." Suddenly she hiked herself up on one elbow and said, "You not like me? You like one of my sisters?"

"No, no! I like you fine. Only—I already have a wife."

"She not here. I here." There was no arguing with that kind of logic. While I was trying to think of something else to say, she put her head back down beside me. I could feel her smiling in the dark. "Now we sleep together. You be mine as long as you stay. No other girl even talk to you."

I thought that one over for a while. Then I decided that there really wasn't so much to think about. I was in Eskimo country and I'd just have to, by God, put up with their customs.

She was already up and stirring when I woke in the morning. I stretched. I felt real good. She brought me a washbasin and towel and, when I was all cleaned up, a steaming cup of coffee. Later, I dressed and went down to the bank where the dogs were tied. The rest of my buddies were there, and all I needed was one look at their faces to know that they had decided to go along with the Eskimo customs, too.

"Hey, Jimmy," one of them yelled, "how'd you sleep?" And they all burst out laughing.

"Okay, okay," I told them, "you're very funny. Now let's take those furs up to the store and get what we came for and get out of here. Otherwise we'll all be hauling Eskimo wives home. That'd be something to laugh about, too, wouldn't it?"

That quieted them down pretty quick. The old man started us up a hard trail to the trading post, and we made it in good time. The trader was a white man married to an Eskimo woman, and he gave us a fair price for our skins. He had milk and just about everything else we needed. I bought a fancy bandanna for Cecelia, but after we had the sleds loaded, I got to thinking and I went back and bought a second bandanna. Then we started back.

We had meant to stop in Kobuk only long enough to say good-bye to our new friends. But before we even got to the town, a group of them came mushing up the trail to meet us, Henry's father in the lead. "You no leave today," he said. "Big storm coming from south."

I looked out over that empty land and, sure enough, rolling up on the horizon was a line of dark gray clouds. You could see that they were loaded with snow.

"By morning nothing move here," he said. "You better stay until storm past. Now we go tie dogs down good."

Well, there wasn't a thing I could do about that. We saw to the dogs, then let some boys talk us into playing in a kind of wild football game. There must have been a hundred people in it—boys and girls, men and women, all fighting for one beat-up caribou-hide ball. In the excitement, I noticed Kitty running along beside me. She said, "Too bad storm make you stay here." She was laughing.

When I quit the game she did, too, and we walked back to the igloo together. I could see that she didn't mean to let me get too far away. Inside, she brushed my mukluks and hung my parka. Then she made me a fine rabbit soup. A man could sure get used to that kind of thing.

"I brought a present for you," I told her. "It's in my parka."

Her eyes went all wide and her face lit up like five candles. She ran to the parka and came back admiring the bandanna, trying it on this way and that way.

"Thank you," she said softly. "Gee, that's good you like me."

There didn't seem to be anything else to do so I crawled back in the bedroll and went to sleep. When I woke up, the girl was sleeping alongside me, as though we'd been married for years and years.

The storm hit during the night, and by morning there was nearly six feet of fresh snow on the ground, and it was still coming down. The old man rigged a line to the igloo, and we managed to get out one last time to make sure the dogs were tied loosely enough so the snow couldn't drift up and smother them. You couldn't see two yards ahead. Without the line, I'd have wandered around all day trying to find my way back. Struggling toward the igloo, I wondered how long we cheechakos from the Indian country would have lasted in this blizzard out on the open tundra.

For five days the wind blew a gale and the snow piled up twice as high as a man's head and, where it drifted, to the size of a mountain. I had never seen anything like that storm, although I guess the Eskimos saw it all the time.

There was nothing to do but stay in the igloo and eat and sleep and tell stories. I told of my mother's long trip through the Eskimo country, and some of them said they remembered hearing about that. I told stories about my hunting trips and about the Yukon River country, and the old man said it was good for the young ones to hear about the Indian's life. He told about how his people lived long ago, and it wasn't very different from the old Indian stories.

Whenever I wanted something—sometimes even before I knew I wanted it—Kitty had it for me. I got to like her real well so it wasn't a bad time. I sure didn't want for anything. If it weren't for worrying about Cecelia and Christine and the people in Cutoff I wouldn't have been in any hurry to get back.

On the sixth day the storm blew itself out. That night I went around and told the other men that we were pulling out first thing in the morning. Some of them weren't any too anxious, but I said that if we stayed any longer we'd all have to go to Fairbanks and get divorces. I said good-bye to the family the night before, but Kitty walked out to the team with me in the pitch-dark dawn.

"I won't forget about you," she said. "If you come back, I be your woman again."

I said I wouldn't forget about her either, and I meant it. The sled moved off and I kept looking back, waving to her. I saw her wave, too. Then she was lost in the darkness.

We really made tracks on the way home. We had been gone two weeks on a trip that should have taken six days, and there is nothing like a guilty conscience to make a man take it out on his dogs. We came mushing into Cutoff the next night. The people were sure glad to see us. We passed out the food and things even before we said hello to our families, so it was real late by the time Cecelia and I had a chance to be alone. Then I gave her the bandanna and she thought that that was just the best present.

She was full of questions. "Was it a good trip? Did anything happen?"

"Not much," I told her, "except for the storm. Hardly anything at all."

CHAPTER FIVE

Dogsled Racing

I KEPT WORKING to build up a stake. Some years I cleared a few dollars trapping; other years I could barely pay for my outfit. One summer I bought an old scow and an older kicker and went freighting along the Koyukuk for a couple of trading posts. But the best I could do going upriver was maybe four miles an hour, and nobody gets rich at that speed. I paid for my gas. That was about it.

Around this time, 1938 and 1939, the people got all interested in dogsled racing again. It had been a big thing around Nome during gold rush days—25,000 people locked into a tarpaper town from October to the June breakup with nothing much else to do for a pastime—but when the gold played out, so did the dog derbies. Now, though, the Natives began taking it up: everybody had dogs, and most of us bragged about them, and pretty soon there was more gambling on the races than there was at poker.

It was no sport for weaklings. Endurance was more important than speed. The trails were a hundred miles and more long and laid out across the toughest terrain we could find to test a team's staying power. You didn't get into the sled unless you were near dead. You ran alongside it the whole way, sometimes sneaking a downhill ride on the runners. But then, going uphill, you had to be ready to push. The rules made it tougher yet. If you started out with twelve dogs, you had to come back with twelve, and many a man packed a lame husky home in the sled. Once a driver left the starting line, he was the only man allowed to lay a hand on his team. I've seen a musher chased up a tree by bears or moose, his dogs scattered to the four winds, and all he ever got was a wave of the hand as the next team went by.

I did pretty well in the races around home. Soon I was competing against the best teams of the other villages, and the men in Cutoff let me take my pick of their dogs. I even won a few big races. But I never thought any more about it than as a way to have fun and maybe pick up fifteen or twenty dollars betting.

Then, in the autumn of 1939, the last mail boat brought real news to Cutoff: some people were setting up a big dogsled race in Fairbanks for the following March. There was to be more than ten thousand dollars in prizes. I was still thinking about that when they handed me a letter from a gold mining outfit. It said that they were willing to pay a thousand dollars for my claims up at Clear Creek, and could I come to Fairbanks and sign the papers?

Could I? I put those two little nuggets of news

together and suddenly they sounded like the answer to all my prayers. If I could add some prize money to my thousand for the claims, I'd have a store ready to open for business in the spring!

I never worked so hard as I did that winter. I borrowed a whole gang of dogs and checked them out and narrowed the bunch down to the best fourteen. Then I got down to some serious training. Day after day I'd hook them to the biggest log I could find and make them pull until their tongues were hanging out. Then it was time to take them out on the flat and build up their speed, and I ran behind that sled until my tongue was hanging out. I shifted the dogs from spot to spot, testing them, getting them used to each other. Back home I pampered them with gruel and milk and the best dried salmon.

All in all, I don't think I got six weeks of trapping in that year. But when February rolled around I was ready to take off for Fairbanks. Most of the people, including Cecelia, thought I was crazy. None of us had ever been to Fairbanks before. It was six hundred miles away, a long way to drive a dog team, and though there were only three thousand people there then, to us it was the big city. What business did a Koyukuk Native have in the big city? Tell the company to send you the papers, they said.

But my heart was set on that race. I thought I had as good a chance of winning as any musher around, and I set off with high hopes. When I got to Ruby on the Yukon, I made camp for a few days. They had fast training trails around there, and I raced those dogs hour after hour. One morning the mail plane came in on the river, an old gull-wing Stinson, and it set me to thinking. I was still five hundred miles from Fairbanks. If I could fly my dogs the rest of the way, they were bound to get there in better shape than if they had to haul the sled overland that distance. And with all the money I had coming, I could surely spare a couple of hundred dollars for the fare.

I walked over and asked the pilot how much he would charge to haul my team and me into Fairbanks. That took him by surprise. These days they fly dog teams everywhere, but the planes were a lot smaller then and I don't think any of them had ever carried that much weight before, and certainly not divided among fourteen dogs. Finally, after counting them three times, he said it would cost a hundred and twenty-five dollars—"if we can get off the ground."

I said if he didn't mind waiting a day or so for the money, it was a deal, and we started right in loading the dogs. Don't think that didn't take a lot of coaxing. They yipped and moaned, and you could just see that old bird settle low on her skis as I chased them aboard, one after another. At the last, we had to take the sled apart to fit it in. Then the pilot cranked her up and we turned out on the ice.

It took a mile before we ever lifted off—and a mile was exactly all the straight Yukon River we had. The trees came rushing up on us and we banked away at the last second. Then we just hung over the ice, with barely enough clearance to follow the bends and turns. We were almost to Kokrines, thirty miles away, before the pilot dared pull back on the stick and lift us up over the trees. And of course once we gained altitude the ride got a little rough and the plane started to bounce and in no time at all we had fourteen dogs being sick along the whole length of the fuselage. The air was so ripe you could have peeled it. The pilot shoved his door open and I did the same, and only that whipping wind in our faces saved the day.

We flew along the river until we were past Tanana, then turned southeast. When we picked up the railroad tracks, just before dark, we followed them right in over a great big ocean of lights. They stretched for miles in every direction, straight strings of them and colored ones, and some that moved along the ground almost as fast as we were moving through the air. This was Fairbanks, and my first look at it left me goggle-eyed. How was a person supposed to find his way in that maze?

We came bumping down to a landing on past the edge of the town. The pilot jumped out even before the propeller stopped turning. He just stood there in the cold dark, breathing deeply. After a while he asked me where I was headed and I said I didn't know. "Well, get your dogs out of there and I'll take you into town. And you better be back out here in the morning to help me clean up that airplane!" He sure sounded mad.

I fumbled around in the dark and finally found a fence and tied the dogs down. No one was happier to be back on the ground than they were. Then I got into an automobile with the pilot and he drove on into the town. I did my best to pick out a landmark or two so I'd know how to get back, but every street looked exactly like the last one: full of big buildings and people scurrying around as though this was their last day on earth. Finally we stopped in front of a place with a big lighted sign hanging off the front of it. The lights spelled out HOTEL. Then they went off. Then they went on again. The pilot said they'd fix me up with a place to stay there. Nervous as a cat, I went in and told the old lady behind the counter what I wanted.

She looked me up and down. I guess I was a sight, still wearing my old bush clothes, and the smell of the dogs all over me. She said, "I don't allow liquor nor women in the rooms after nine o'clock."

Man, that really embarrassed me. "No, ma'am," I said. "I don't either."

She asked me for ten dollars for the night or thirty dollars for the week—in advance. I poked around in my pants and pulled out my stake. The whole thing came to less than fifty dollars, and the race was still nearly a month off. But what could I do? I handed over the thirty dollars and said a little prayer that those mining people had my thousand dollars ready.

The room had a nice soft bed, and if you climbed some steps there was a shower with warm water. Once I was cleaned up, I went back again and asked the lady where I could get something to eat—I hadn't eaten since breakfast. She said in any café, so I started down the street, making sure I didn't lose sight of that big blinking HOTEL sign. I passed two places that said RESTAURANT and one that said EATS, but I figured I had to find a cafe. Cars went by this way and that way, and I took no chances. Whenever I came to a corner, I would make sure that there wasn't a car in sight, and I'd run across the street as though something were after me.

Then I came to a store with two naked women in the window. I just looked up and there they were—naked as the day they were born!—and I got so flustered I ran right out among the cars and almost got myself killed. Horns honked and people yelled at me, and I ran all the faster, my head hung in shame and my poor brain twirling from the struggle to figure out what the hell was going on in this town. I even forgot about the blinking HOTEL sign and turned a corner, trying to get as far from those women as I could. When I finally got the nerve to look up again, I was hopelessly lost.

I kept going. But now no matter which way I turned, nothing looked familiar. I began to worry about the dogs.

What would happen to them if I couldn't find my way back? I also began to get dizzy with hunger—it was past ten o'clock now—and when I came to a place where I could look through the window and see some people sitting at a counter and eating, I stopped. I was just standing there staring in when a man came out and looked me over. "Hungry, pal?" he asked.

I said I hadn't eaten since the morning, and he tried to give me some money. I told him I had money. I just didn't know what to do in a place like that.

He almost fell down laughing and I had my fist all clenched to lay him out on the sidewalk when he caught hold of himself and said, "First time in from the bush, huh? Well, just go right in there and tell the waitress what you want—steak or ham and eggs or anything—and they'll cook it up for you."

I told him thanks and went in and sat up to the counter. I felt like all knees and elbows. The waitress put a glass of water in front of me, so I drank it. Then she gave me a two page book but I couldn't make much sense out of it, so when she came back and asked me what I wanted I said steak.

"What kind?" she said.

"Any kind."

She sure gave me a dirty look. She was a real pretty girl, all dressed in white, and I hated to have her mad at me.

"What do you mean, 'Any kind'?" she said. "We have rib steak, sirloin..."

"Yeah, *that* kind—rib steak."

"Rare, medium, or well-done?"

"Medium." I was sure glad I got *that* right, whatever it meant.

Pretty soon she came back with a plateful of potatoes and vegetables and a little piece of meat. Not only was it little, but it didn't seem hardly dead, there was that much blood running off it. She must have thought I wanted it raw. I didn't want to hurt her feelings so I ate it. Actually, once I got the hang of eating without looking at my plate, it wasn't half bad. She asked if I wanted some pie and I said okay. Then I put a five-dollar bill down and she took it away and brought me change, ten cents. I didn't know whether to laugh or cry—I could have lived off the store shelf in Cutoff for a week on what I'd just spent!

I went out and tried to figure out a way to find the hotel. Finally I decided to do the same thing a man does in the bush when he's lost: walk in a widening circle until he sees something familiar. I went all the way around one block, then another and another. After a while I came to the main street and there, way down, was the HOTEL sign. I was sure relieved to see it. Then I came to that store with the naked women in it. I was still too bashful to walk past them, so I had to go back to the corner and cross over. I couldn't figure out what in the world those women were doing there. I'd heard there were places like that in Fairbanks, but you wouldn't think they'd let them stand right in front of a big lighted window.

It was mighty lonesome going up to that room alone. I fiddled around for a while, then decided I'd walk out and see my dogs. I went down and asked the old lady how to get out to the airport. She said it was five miles but I didn't care. I started out and found it without too much trouble. The dogs were sure glad to see me. I guess they felt as strange in that place as I did. I wished I had some feed for them, but I hadn't brought any and there was no place to buy it at that hour of the night. Anyhow, they were all right, so I fooled with them for a while, then went back and went to bed. I'd sure learned a lot that first day. I remember thinking: well, I've paid for my first meal and my first bed and one thing was for sure—I wasn't going to eat steak very darned often.

Next morning, I moved the dogs down by some willows along the Chena River. That was a lot closer to town and I could run them on the ice. Then I went back out to the airport and helped the pilot clean the plane. I showed him the letter from the mining company and he said he would drive me there in his automobile. On the way into town I asked him if he knew what those women were doing in that store window on the main street.

"What women?" he said.

"Well, they just stand there in that window and they — oh, never mind."

The mining outfit was in another one of those big buildings but the people seemed glad to see me. They brought out a whole bundle of papers for me to sign, and I made believe I was reading them but the truth is I couldn't make head or tail out of what they were supposed to say. I just asked if I got the thousand dollars when I signed and they said yes, so I signed.

They counted out the bills—man, they felt good piling up in my palm—and then one of them asked if I was reporting to the Internal Revenue department. I said I didn't know what that was, so they told me it was the outfit that collects taxes for the government, and that I had to go right over there. "Lucky for you their office is right in this building," they said.

Very lucky. At this Internal Revenue place they asked me a swarm of questions about how much money I had and how much I'd made on my freighting operation. They had me sign another batch of papers and then it was their turn to hold out a palm. I said how come, and they told me that Uncle Sam took part of the money that everybody made. That was taxes. I said that Uncle Sam had a pretty good deal there and I wished I'd thought of it first. When I left, there was a serious dent in my thousand dollars.

Outside, the pilot was waiting for his hundred and a quarter. By the time I got back to my room and counted what I had left, I figured I might be eating dried fish and sleeping with the dogs before I got out of Fairbanks. There was only one good thing. On the way back I'd sneaked a look across the street at those women. They were still there but at least now they had some clothes on.

In the next few days some of the other mushers came in from the bush so I had somebody to talk to besides the dogs. I didn't spend too much time with the mushers because they liked to go out drinking and looking for women, and I figured I'd already wasted enough money. By day I was out on the river ice—running my dogs, and by night I was getting my thirty-dollars-a-week's worth at that hotel. I was usually asleep by eight-thirty. In between, I ate hotcakes and hash, and watched my pile of dollars get smaller and smaller.

One afternoon, though, when we'd all been out on the trail and were sitting around on the bank of the Chena and they were talking about their favorite subject—women —I said that I knew where there were some women who were available. The way they looked at me reminded me of the time I'd brought the white mule to Cutoff. Then they all jumped up and said, "Let's go!" So I tied up my dogs and led them back to town. "They're right up in the middle of this street," I said when we got to the corner.

"Aren't you coming?"

"Not me."

I watched them trying to keep from running. I saw them look where I'd told them, then at each other, then back at me. Then they started walking toward the corner again. They sure looked disgusted. "What's the matter?" I asked. "Wouldn't they let you in?"

One of them said, "What are you—funny or crazy?"

Another one spoke up: "I say crazy." And they all walked off.

I stood there for a minute, as mixed up as I've ever been. People kept walking by all the time, and it didn't seem to bother them any. Finally I got up my nerve and went right up there without stopping. The women were there, all right; in the window. At first I thought that they were dead and just propped up there. Then I looked closer and saw that they were just dummies, wooden models, long skinny things with paint on their faces and fake hair. Don't think I didn't feel a real long way from my little cabin on the Hogatza at that minute. Crazy was right.

By the time the day of the race rolled around, I was sure ready to go home. All I wanted was to take a piece of that prize money and get back on the trail. I still felt confident. Some of the boys from the Yukon villages were pretty good mushers but there was prize money for the first five places and only fifteen teams entered. Even if I finished fifth I'd collect two hundred and fifty dollars.

I knew it was a rough course before I started—nearly ninety miles north over an unbroken trail to the mining camp at Livengood, an overnight layover, then back— but not until I was actually out on the trail did I realize what I was in for. We went down into ravines and up out again, over mountains and through brush that tried to snag you on every turn and often did. It was the toughest race I've ever been in, before or since, and by the time I was ten miles out I figured I'd be lucky to get my team back to Fairbanks, let alone win anything. Four of my dogs had gone lame on me during training so I only had ten pulling. It wasn't near enough for that country.

But I wasn't about to quit. I'd come too far and spent too much to give up without an honest try. I pushed those dogs for all they were worth and I hardly ever set foot on the runners. Then, practically into Livengood, we came down a slope so steep that the brakes wouldn't hold and the sled went smashing into the two dogs on the end of the team. Their hind paws were so banged up that they could hardly walk. They surely wouldn't be pulling for a while, so I undid the harness and packed them into the sled. Before I could get going again, another team passed me.

Still, when we got to the roadhouse in Livengood, I found out I was in fifth place. That perked me up: maybe by morning the tail-enders would be able to run again. I saw to the dogs, then went over to have something to eat. There hadn't been so much excitement around Livengood since they found the gold. Three times the town's normal population of one hundred was squirming around to find breathing room in that roadhouse, a radio announcer was telling all about the race—that was the first time that a dogsled race was ever broadcast on the radio, so you can see what a big deal it was—and everybody was trying to buy the mushers a drink. The only thing I had to say to them was, "No, thanks." I finally managed to get a hamburger and some tea, but I had to fight my way outside to eat it. I checked the dogs one more time, then went up to a big barn of a room above the roadhouse where the mushers were supposed to sleep. I should have stayed with the dogs. The drunks made such a racket downstairs that even when I dozed off it seemed as though the carrying-on was happening inside my head.

Then it was two a.m. and time to get up for the run back. I didn't want to go back down to that drunken jamboree so I went right out to the dogs without breakfast or coffee or anything. I didn't have too much time: we were to leave at two-minute intervals and my team would be fifth out of the starting chute. The hurt dogs were still limping badly so I packed them in the sled and we rode out into the cold pitch-dark, the dogs following the trail and running hard.

By the time the sky began to lighten off to the left, I was beginning to think that maybe I had that fifth-place finish clinched. There was no sign of anybody behind me and even with the extra load in the sled the team was still strong and eager. And once, from the top of a long hill, I saw the musher up ahead. He was only a mile or so away.

But we ran into trouble. We were better than halfway home now and the strain was beginning to tell. The dogs stumbled and every time I stopped yelling at them they looked back to see if it was time to stop. Then we came to a steep killer of a hill, and hard as I pushed on the sled they just couldn't make it up. Their paws skittered out from under them and they yipped and pulled but just weren't getting anywhere. That's when I made my big decision: I chased the two lame dogs out of the sled and made them walk up the hill. If they took off somewhere I'd be disqualified. But if they stuck with us, we were okay, for without that extra 180 pounds of weight, the team could get the sled up. At the top of the hill I held my breath and looked back. And there came the cripples, limping along after us as hard as they could. I gave them each a big squeeze and put them back in the sled, and away we went downhill. And that's how we managed to get back to Fairbanks.

Coming down into the flats, not five miles from the finish line, I realized that we were closing in on the team ahead. I pushed those dogs for all I was worth, coaxing and hollering: there was a five-hundred-dollar prize for the fourth-place team, and suddenly five hundred dollars seemed like all the money in the world to me. "Come on! Come on! Run!" I called. And they ran. Little by little we crawled up on them. We came as close as a hundred yards—but that was it. The musher up there had ten healthy dogs pulling and I could hear him giving them what-for as we ran into the edge of the town. Now we were on the main street, not ten blocks from the finish line and I figured, well, that was a nice dream, but I'd just have to be satisfied with two hundred and fifty. It would pay for an airplane to take us home and leave me a little something for all the weeks of work.

Then a funny thing happened. We went by a gasoline station, and the dogs up ahead took a sudden shine to a bright red pump. With the poor driver cursing and threatening them every inch of the way, they galloped right up to the gas station, circled the pump once, twice, three times, and were still hopelessly tangled as I ran by with the fourth place sewed up.

Everybody made a big fuss over the winners. They wanted to buy us drinks and dinner, and a radio announcer kept calling us over to his microphone. All I wanted was to take a shower and go to bed. I eased myself out of the crowd, tied the dogs and fed them, and went back to the hotel. I didn't wake up until eleven the following morning. When I went to the Chena to see my dogs I found out that half the teams weren't in yet.

I didn't plan to stay in Fairbanks an hour more than I had to. I went right over to the manager's tent and told him I'd come for my prize money. You never saw a sadder-looking creep. "Jimmy," he said, "there is no money."

I figured I hadn't heard him right. I said, "I won fourth place. I got five hundred dollars coming..."

"There was barely enough to pay off the first three teams. The rest of the money never came in. We're broke."

"But you let all of us run. We ran all that way..."

All of a sudden I felt more played out than when I'd finished the race. The thousand for my gold claims was almost all gone and that five hundred dollars meant everything to me. Maybe I could still start the store with that much, or save it until I could lay my hands on some more. And now...

"We thought the sponsors would come through," he was saying. "We thought with the race on and all the excitement, they'd put up the rest of the money they'd promised and we could pay everybody off." He shook his head from side to side. "But they didn't."

For a white-hot minute I figured I had to take it out of his hide. A man ought to have some way to unload the raging disappointment I felt. But I guess there isn't enough white man in me. The Indian, you see, only knows how to suffer in silence. So I turned around and walked out of there. The dogs were waiting, all harnessed and ready to go. We had a long, hard six hundred miles ahead of us. I wondered if it was long enough for me to get the stink of Fairbanks out of my system.

There was a lot of excitement in Cutoff on December 7, 1941. Somebody had one of those battery radios, and it kept telling how the Japanese had bombed Pearl Harbor in Hawaii. Everyone said they'd be heading for Alaska next, right up the Aleutian chain. Some of the younger fellows even went out on the bank and stood there looking west into the sky.

I didn't pay much attention. My wife was sick, very sick, and there just didn't seem to be room in my head to worry about anything else. The Jap navy could have come sailing up the Koyukuk River and, the way I felt that afternoon, if they didn't bother Cecelia I wouldn't have bothered them.

She had got sick after freeze-up and a doctor came and said she had TB. There was nothing much to do, he said, just hope. Well, hoping didn't help either. She got worse and worse, and that night—December 7, 1941—she died. I sat with her for a long time. My Uncle Johnny had the baby, and I'd shooed everyone else out. So I just sat there, trying to figure out what I was going to do now and wondering if Cecelia was watching me from somewhere, happier maybe.

As soon as she was buried, I took off for the winter cabin at Hogatza. Uncle Johnny and his wife were looking after Christine so there was nothing to keep me, and all at once I felt a deep-down urge to be a long way from people.

I worked very hard. Every day that a creature could move I was out on the trap line or hunting bear for Cecelia's potlatch. But it was all different now. For the first time in my life I knew what it was to be lonely.

It seemed to be better when I came in from the bush in the spring. I spent a lot of time with Christine, and there was plenty to keep me busy—getting ready for the potlatch, whipsawing lumber to fix up Cecelia's grave. But when all that was done the same loneliness took hold of me, and a kind of restlessness that pushed me from place to place and made me dissatisfied with everyplace. Then I heard that the Army was looking for men to raft gasoline from the railhead at Nenana down the Tanana and Yukon to a new air base at Galena. I got my scow in shape and signed up, and all that summer and every summer until the war was over I hauled gasoline to Galena. One more time I started to build up a stake. One more time I took to daydreaming about running my own trading post.

In the autumn of 1943, 1 began going with a girl named Dorothy Frank. Quite a few of the girls in Cutoff had been making up to me and it wasn't because I was rich or handsome. My attraction was being single and not spoken for. But Dorothy seemed different. She always made a big fuss over Christine, and said right out that a little girl like that should have a mother. Still, I wasn't about to rush out and buy the cow when milk was so cheap, so when the time came I said I'd see her in the spring and went off to trap.

Well, there's nothing like being alone in the bush for six months to start a man thinking. I came to believe that it wasn't fair to leave Christine with friends or relatives every winter. She did need a mother. And maybe I needed a woman to settle me down again. And there wasn't anything wrong with Dorothy Frank. So when spring came we were married and lived together for twelve years and had seven children. She was a good wife all that time, and a good mother—to Christine, too, who was part of our family—and to this day I can't find it in my heart to say anything bad about her. Why did she walk out on us? I wish I really knew. But anyway, that's getting ahead of the story.

I don't know what happened to those years. They just flew by. One day the house was full of babies and then all of a sudden the girls were fussing with their hair and mooning over store dresses, and the older boys were putting out their own beaver sets. I still did a lot of trapping and, in summer, freighted supplies along the river in a new boat I'd built.

One year I missed out on a big shipment because the fur buyer who brought the letter telling me about it couldn't get to Cutoff until it was too late to do the job. That made me mad enough to sit down and write to the territorial governor and to the man in Washington, D.C., who was supposed to be our representative. The buyer carried the letters out for me, and by June we had a post office. Cutoff was on the map and would get mail every week that a plane could land on the river.

It seemed to be so easy, after all the years we'd been without one, that it made me take a good long look around our whole village. It was as though I had been blind before and was seeing Cutoff for the first time, and what I saw made me sick. It was a dirty little place, set on a piece of low ground that reeked of swampy water the summer long, dogs tied close to the houses and the walks littered with everybody's garbage.

But the thing that bothered me most was that we had

no school. I had four kids by then, and another on the way, and I knew the difference between a Native who had a little learning and one who had none. Learning gave you the right to hope for something better. Without it you had a one-way ticket to nowhere, a guarantee that you'd leave this life without a single good reason for having been here. So that summer I made a special trip to Fairbanks to see the bishop of our church. I asked him to get the commissioner of education to build us a school.

"Jimmy," he said, "there is no decent place to build a school in Cutoff. The land is too wet. It isn't healthy."

"What if I talk people into moving to higher ground?"

He thought that one over for a while. Then he said, "If you could do that, I think the commissioner would see things our way."

Of course I hadn't told him that the only high ground around Cutoff was the cemetery hill, eighteen miles away on the Huslia River. Everybody knows that my people are very superstitious about the dead. But I thought if I moved out there first, others might follow. One thing for sure, the bishop was right: every thaw the river flooded and half the kids came down with fever, and the whole village smelled bad until first frost.

Next spring, as soon as the ice went out, I cut new logs and rafted them down the river. A few of the younger men helped me, and we winched the logs up on the bank, about a quarter of a mile above the cemetery, and I began to work on a new house. As the days grew longer I worked on into the night, staying right there as long as my supplies lasted. Then, when I'd go back to Cutoff, the people would say, "Ha ha. Did you wake the dead? Did you see any ghosts?" They pretended to be kidding but they weren't.

"No," I'd tell them, "I didn't see any ghosts. But I saw lots of good dry wood for winter right up on the bank."

Pretty soon some other men made up their minds to go along with me, and tore down their old houses and floated the logs downriver. Then old Grandpa, the medicine man, said he would come, and of course lots of families followed him. We marked off a nice piece of ground for each home site, fifty feet on each side of the cabin, with plenty of room behind for a cache and a proper outhouse. We made it a rule that all the dogs had to be tied down out beyond the last house.

"I'm tired of living in a dirty village," I said. "We have a chance now to build a nice clean one. Let's not spoil it."

My wife thought it was all foolishness. "What's wrong with the place we've got?" she said, and wouldn't even come down to look at the new house until it was finished.

The trader gave me a hard time, too. He was a white man, old and cranky, and he didn't want to start building a new store. He said I was only stirring up trouble. He even sent word to the marshal that I was planning to run a gambling game in the new village, and they sent for me to come to Fairbanks, and I had to go all the way down there to tell the marshal it wasn't so. As long as I was there I told him something else: "If that old man won't move his store where the people want to live, we'll build a store of our own. Then he can go crying to the governor." Pretty soon the trader changed his mind and came downriver asking who would help him build a new store, and we all did.

We named our new village Huslia, after the river. Not long after we were settled in, Wien Airlines came and said they'd fly in twice a week if we helped them build a runway. So I freighted their cat and grader down the river, and in six weeks a bunch of us had packed down a nice 4,500-foot strip. Now we had regular air service, too.

That summer my uncle, Hog River Johnny, died. He had been blind for many years, but he was the last of the real old-time Native hunters, and the people respected him. It was a very big loss to me. He had taught me so much, and now there were no more of my mother's people left and it seemed as though a whole way of life was behind me. Who knew what was ahead?

I made up my mind that Johnny was going to have a potlatch to be proud of and went out and shot a bear and a nice bull moose. Some of the other men got some ducks, so when we cooked up the washtubs of meat there was plenty to feed the whole town. I had got word to my brother Sidney, who was working in the gold mines up the Hogatza, and he came down. After the meal we sat and talked about Johnny and our Dad and the old days.

Since he'd come down for the potlatch, Sidney decided to stay and visit for a few days. That's why I've always figured that Uncle Johnny left us all a great gift, although it was an accident and he would never know about it. Sidney was walking along the riverbank one morning and, having a good eye for such things, he noticed clear water seeping into the silty flow of the Huslia. "I think there's fresh water under your town, Jimmy," he said. "I think you can tap it."

We went to Fairbanks and bought point and pipes and began driving a well. Now there are very few places in our part of the country where you can do that. Mostly the ground is rock-hard with permafrost. Here, though, using a spring line with a hundred-pound log on end, we punched slowly through. Sidney and I would pull on the line until the log was raised up over the head of the pipe. Then we'd let go. Smash, and the pipe would sink down another half-inch. In a week we were sixty feet down, and there we hit a steady flow of fresh water.

Do you know what that meant to my people? For the first time in our lives we had running water, good water. We didn't have to pack it up from the river anymore, where it ran muddy and foul every time there was a frost or a thaw. It was a blessing. Soon nearly everyone had driven a well. The people were healthier, cleaner.

Finally the bishop brought the commissioner of education to see our new town. They both looked around and I suppose they liked what they saw: we soon had three thousand dollars to buy lumber, windows, and doors for the new school. Of course we had to supply logs and labor, but that was no trouble. By freeze-up we had a nice snug building and a teacher for the twenty-four kids in the village.

It took a while to round up all twenty-four. Some were sixteen and older and had never seen the inside of a schoolhouse. They decided they were too old to start now. A few of us persuaded them otherwise. Also there were men who took their families out to winter cabins and trap lines, same as they'd always done, and we had to go chasing into the bush to remind them that their kids were supposed to be in school. Not one of them complained.

In a few years the population of Huslia was twice what we'd started with, one hundred and eighty people. They quit dying of fever and TB, and when a new baby was born we didn't have to sweat out whether it was going to live or die. I guess word of this got outside: after a while teams of doctors all the way from Chicago and New York were coming around to make tests and ask us questions, and the

Army did a study that showed Huslia to be the healthiest village in the whole Yukon Valley.

Of course I was proud of my part in starting up the new town. But it was hard work and took a lot of time, and it hadn't put a penny in my pocket. Fur was bringing less and less, and practically nobody went hunting it anymore. The people got on relief and made out just as well. Where once the whole country had lived off the trap line, now only two men in all Huslia bothered. I was one of them. I just didn't see how a healthy man could take money for laying around and doing nothing.

But my catch was barely paying for my outfit anymore, and I was sure ready to try something different. That's why, when Don Stickman, a Native bush pilot I knew from the old days in Nulato, asked me to go bounty hunting with him I said yes without thinking twice. He came flying into Huslia with his Super Cub on skis early one winter, and told me we could make some real money going after wolves. The Territory was paying a fifty-dollar bounty for each hide, he said, and lots of guys had made a killing hunting from the air. He'd do the flying if I'd do the shooting, and once we'd paid the plane expenses we could split the rest, pure profit. We just had to take a hundred hides, he said, it was that easy.

The one thing he forgot to say was that the only bounty hunting anyone had ever heard of before was up on the open arctic slope. Chasing wolves through this timber country was a different breed of cat. Nobody had ever even tried it before. By the end of two days I knew why. Once you spotted a wolf, you chased it at treetop height, maybe sometimes a little below, and then you landed in the nearest postage stamp sized clearing you could find to skin it out.

The way I figured it, the wolf was only slightly worse off than we were.

But we were getting our fair share of hides. The word got out and pretty soon there were other planes bounty hunting, lots of them. And I thought, well, if all these people are doing it, it can't be so dangerous. And so, although airplane flying is not my idea of a good time, especially when you're brushing branches out of your eyes half the time, I concentrated very hard on the stake I was building up and popped away at every wolf we tracked down.

The pilots have a way of describing a crackup. They call it buying the farm. Well, Stickman and I didn't buy the farm, but it sure looked as though we were making down payments. Once we landed on the side of a mountain—a place where no one who cared anything about his own skin would be chasing a wolf—and we had to jump out and hang onto the wings before the plane slid all the way back down. We took off going downhill—that was the only way—and it was like trying to pull up out of a full power dive. Before we finally did, we came close enough to that valley floor to stir up a snowstorm with our prop wash.

Another time we got a wolf alongside a little creek and landed on the pond it fed into. I don't know how Stickman put the plane into that spot: it wasn't big enough to hold a respectable hockey game. Getting out seemed plain impossible. After we'd found the wolf and skinned him out, Stickman, who usually sees the bright side of things, said it looked a little tight. I said it certainly did and that it would take a can opener to get us out of there.

Then he got the idea of cutting down some trees on the far side of the pond to give us a little more takeoff room. After we'd cut trees for an hour, he took a good hard look and said that if we pulled the plane as far back up on the slope of the bank as we could, he thought we could make it. I thought he was crazy, but it was either his way or trying to walk out, and it was forty miles to the nearest human being. I started pulling.

Once we got the plane back another twenty feet or so, Stickman gave me very careful instructions. I was to hang on to the tail with one hand and a tree with the other so the plane wouldn't start sliding down before he was ready. Just before he gunned the motor, he would yell to me, then I was supposed to jump in. I said okay and got a good grip on the tail. I also said a little prayer that went something like, "Please, God, make sure You've given him at least as much sense as You did brass!"

I don't know what happened. Maybe Stickman yelled and I didn't hear him. Or maybe in the excitement he got mixed up. Anyway, the next thing I knew the motor was revved up full blast and the plane was moving and I had a big decision to make: I could let go of the tail or I could let go of the tree because if I held on to both I had a good chance of losing an arm. I let go of both and ran for the open cabin door, diving in just as the plane got up a real head of steam and went bouncing off the slope and onto the ice, full throttle. And there I was as we lifted off and strained to get a little altitude, legs thrashing in air and struggling to climb in. I could have sworn I kicked a couple of treetops. Between my legs, I could see them looming above us as we flew down the swath we'd cut, and I could feel the plane lurch as Stickman threw the nose down over the creek to pick up some flying speed before we stalled out. Fighting the wind, which was trying real hard to pluck me out of there, and Stickman, who kept offering me his hand when all I wanted was for him to keep both his damn hands on the controls, I finally managed to crawl up onto my seat and slam the door shut. When I looked out, we were two hundred feet up and climbing and Stickman was saying, "Gee, I was scared there for a minute." A fat lot he knew: I stayed scared for a week.

That did it. Oh, I finished out the season, and we wound up with a hundred and eighteen skins, but then I told Stickman that he'd have to find himself another hero for next year. Bounty hunting, I decided, was not for me. Either you'd plow up the landscape with your teeth and fingernails, which is what happened to the men in three separate airplanes that year, or you'd grow old too fast worrying that you were about to.

When we'd paid for our gasoline and divided the pot, I had almost two thousand dollars. I could have started up a trading post then and there, right in Huslia. The white trader had died and some people came to me and said, "You open a store here, Jimmy. We need a store here."

But I figured two thousand wasn't quite enough, I needed a little more, just a little bit more. I'd put in one more summer of freighting, I decided, and by freeze-up I'd have enough to lay in a really good stock of supplies. That's what I did. And it was going so well, I had so much business, that I let them talk me into expanding my operation. I leased a big outfit and put on three men—and proved to myself, once and for all, that I had about as much business sense as a bull moose. I was always hauling a load, but my rigs were just too slow to make any real money, and the wages I had to pay slowly bled me white. Anyway, by the time the river froze and I had a chance to sit down and add it all up, my money was gone and what's more I was in the hole for another couple of thousand.

That was a bad time around the Huntington house, that autumn of 1956. 1 was forty years old and further from my life's ambition than I'd ever been. I kept trying to figure out what it all meant. Was it a sign that I ought to give up and quit trying? Should I be satisfied to live out my days like the other people, taking what came and not dreaming of anything more? If that was so then I was in for a lot of unhappiness because I just couldn't accept it. There had to be a way for me. There had to.

I was all set to go back up to Hogatza when some of the men came to me and asked if I'd consider having another shot at the dogsled races. They offered to lend me any of their dogs that I wanted, and to make up a pot of money that would at least get me to Anchorage or Fairbanks and back. The races had become really big-time by now. The Alaskan Championship was the high point of the Fur Rendezvous in Anchorage every February, and the North American Dogsled Derby was the number-one event in the Fairbanks Winter Carnival soon after. To Alaskans, both of them were like the World Series and the Irish Sweepstakes put together, with the very best mushers from all over the Territory and a few from the South 48 competing. People talked about the races all year, and when they were on you couldn't get a lick of work out of anyone within reach of a radio or TV.

I didn't know what to say. I could understand why these men were after me to do it. It would make them feel more a part of the races. Their dogs and someone they knew would be in it, and they would hear the announcers say the name of Huslia. But what about me? I was fifteen years past the best age for dogsled racing, and I hadn't completely gotten the bad taste of that last try in Fairbanks out of my mouth. And yet, there was the store, a picture so clear in my head I could all but reach out and touch it. If I won...

I thought it over for two days and then went to the men and said I would have a try at putting a team together. If it looked good by February first I would go to Anchorage. Otherwise I'd return the dogs they'd loaned me and we could forget the whole thing.

Next morning, I started training. They brought me twenty dogs, and I used my own best three. Out of them all, I hoped to get a decent team of twelve and a couple of extras, and the first thing I did was to weed out the weak ones. Both the Anchorage and Fairbanks races are run in three heats on successive days. I set my training runs the same way, twenty-five miles a day for two days, forty miles the third day. Then I let the dogs rest for two days. There was no rest for me. When a man gets to be forty years old his body is not so willing to do the hard work needed to get it in shape. It takes longer and becomes a form of punishment. Yet my condition was just as important as the dogs', and if I let a day go by without toughening myself it would take me two days to get back to where I was. So every morning I ran three miles before breakfast and did the same in the afternoon, this time pushing the sled. Sometimes I put my little boy Wayne in it to make the run tougher. I jumped rope twice a day, fifteen minutes each time, watched what I ate, and quit smoking. It was brutally hard to make myself do all that, but in a month I was down to a bone-hard hundred and forty-seven pounds and felt as though I could lick my weight in wildcats.

The team was shaping up, too. With the cripples and weaklings gone, I had fourteen good dogs that pulled hard together and did what I told them. I had one problem, and I was afraid it might be a big one. Monkey, who had always been my lead dog, was getting old. He was just as smart and tried just as hard, but he didn't really have the strength any more to set the kind of fast pace that is called for in a major race. I hated to pull him out. A good lead dog means everything: he is the one who follows the trail and answers the driver's commands, and the other dogs just do what he does. Besides, I felt a little sentimental about Monkey. We had been together a long time and, after all, I was old too. I finally compromised by taking him out of the lead harness and putting him back near the end of the team where he wouldn't have to work so hard. You could see that he was puzzled by this and not too happy. He kept looking at me and whimpering. But good dog that he was, when I yelled, "Go!" he dug right in and ran. Then I went to work training my new lead dog.

By February first I was well satisfied with the team. On the fifteenth, I loaded them on the mail plane and we took off for Fairbanks, on the first leg of the trip to Anchorage, where the Alaskan Championship was scheduled for a week later. The people had collected all they could for my fare, but it was only enough to get me to Fairbanks. I thanked them and said I'd make my own way from there somehow. What I did was to go to a used-car lot, pick out a '51 Ford pickup, and make a deal with the owner. I told him that if I won any of the first three places, I'd come back and pay him $700, which was more than the rig was worth. If I didn't, I'd just return it to him with my best wishes.

Getting the pickup turned out to be the easiest part. I

knew I had to have a driver's license, so I went to the police station, and an officer got in the cab to see how I could do. Since the only things I'd ever driven before were cats and bulldozers, I didn't do too well. Once, halfway through a stoplight, I hit the brakes so hard that I almost put the poor man through the windshield. I think the only reason he gave me a license was because I was a musher on my way to the big race. "Better be real careful for a week or so," he said. He seemed happy to get out.

I put a plywood house on the back for the dogs and left early next morning to beat the traffic out of town. I had nearly four hundred and fifty miles to go. For a while things went fine, although I stuck to my own speed and every other car on the road passed me as though I were standing still. I stopped at Big Delta for a cup of coffee and stood at the junction reading the road signs for a long time. Then I promptly took the wrong turn. I had gone about fifty miles when I came to where some men were plowing through a snow slide in a mountain pass. Chatting with them as I waited to get by, I found out I was headed for Tok, not Anchorage, and had to go all the way back to the junction.

That really put me in a fine mood. I tromped down on the gas pedal and made tracks back to Big D. By the time I got on the right road, I was not only mad, but had all the confidence in the world in my driving and was kicking up quite a snow cloud as I sped along. When I caught up with an Army convoy, I didn't even hesitate about pulling out to pass it, and that was another mistake. Army convoys can stretch out forever: when I had passed twenty trucks in this one I still couldn't see the front of it. Meanwhile, I was in the wrong lane of a two-lane road and halfway up a blind hill, and only luck had kept me in one piece this far. Well, my luck didn't last. A car came zooming up over the top of the hill and I just had time to yank that wheel over and turn off into the ditch. Snow flew every which way and the pickup slowly laid down on its side.

I scrambled out of there. I was positive I'd really had it this time. The pickup looked as though it was settled in for winter, and I knew I could never drive the dogs to Anchorage in time. But the last couple of trucks in the convoy stopped and the GI's, after giving me a good roasting for driving like a cowboy, helped me get the dogs out and tied down. They hooked a chain onto one of the trucks, turned the pickup right side up, and hauled it back on the road.

I was certainly grateful to those boys. Once I'd brushed some snow off the motor and poured a couple of quarts of oil in, I was ready to go—and this time I stayed a respectable distance behind the convoy.

I made a camp in a nice patch of timber where there were plenty of spruce boughs for the dogs' beds, and rolled into Anchorage the next day just after dark. That town made me seem as puny as my first trip to Fairbanks, only more so because Anchorage is a lot bigger. There was a good thick snow falling so that ten feet in front of me all I could see was a brightly lit fog and an endless stream of cars going by on the other side. The streets were piled high with snowbanks. At every corner, a scurrying mob of people pushed in front of the pickup and behind it, and I was sure I was going to kill somebody before I got out of that teeming mess.

As it turned out, I came close to killing myself. Gawking around trying to spot a quiet street or a place to stay, I took my eyes off the car in front of me just long enough to go plowing into his rear end when he stopped for a light. He came swarming back at me, yanked my door open, and in a few thousand well-heated words proceeded to tell me where drivers like me belonged. I didn't say anything. I just sat there staring straight ahead, listening to the lecture and the horns honking behind us and wishing there was some way I could disappear from the face of the earth for an hour or so.

Finally we pulled around to a side street and parked and it turned out there was hardly any damage to either car. Then he realized that I was a musher, and his whole attitude changed. Suddenly he was my best friend. He told me about a nice inexpensive place to stay just outside town where I could keep the dogs right with me, and he showed me exactly how to get there. And when I came back into town next day, after a good night's sleep, darned if he wasn't looking for me on Fourth Avenue to lead me along the streets the racecourse followed out of town.

I could see that was going to be a big problem. It was a mile and a half through the city before the trail came into open country, and I didn't know how my dogs were going to do running through the clatter and crowds of people that would be watching. Nor was the rest of the course any breeze. It crossed several main highways, and though all traffic is stopped on race day, open roads are very tempting to dog teams, and you can easily find yourself going the wrong way. Then it went over a couple of bogs and well up into the foothills of the Chugach Mountain range before turning back to town.

The trail was every team's headache, but I had one of my very own. On the night before the first heat, thirty-two mushers were entered in the race—the largest field ever—

and when we drew lots for starting positions, I came up with number thirty-one. That meant the trail would be all chewed up by the time I got out. Even worse, I was going to have my hands full holding my dogs while they watched thirty other teams take off ahead of them.

When I came into town next morning, it looked as though they were giving away free money. I had never seen so many thousands of people in my life. The sidewalks were packed tight all the way down Fourth Avenue, and men were running out into the street to take pictures, and the poor dogs—mine and everybody else's—went crazy with excitement. I hung onto the towline for all I was worth, trying to calm my team and thinking that I'd never be able to hold them down for the hour or more we had to wait until it was our turn to start. If they didn't break loose, they were bound to start fighting with one another. And if one of those crazy camera bugs wandered close enough they'd chew him down to the knees.

Then some lady came out of the crowd and asked if she could help me. I told her to stand on the brake, which gave me a chance to go up and tell those dogs a thing or two. I never saw that lady again, but she was certainly a friend in need, and I've always been sorry I didn't get to thank her. Maybe she'll read this and remember.

A hundred years later the announcer called out: "Jimmy Huntington, the Huslia Hustler!" and we came tearing down that starting chute like a bolt of lightning. The dogs were just about wild now, and I knew that until we got out from between those masses of people I was just along for the ride and my big job was to hang on.

It was quite a job. We hadn't gone five blocks when somebody shot off one of those flashguns at us and the team got scared and wheeled right into the crowd, climbed the sidewalk and swerved left again barely in time to keep from splashing me through a plate glass shop window. If I were just watching it all I'd have laughed myself silly at the looks on the faces of those people as they scrambled out of our way, some of them diving over each other and others upended as the dogs bolted straight ahead along the building line. I knew I couldn't stop them now, and if I tried to turn them back out into the street there was every chance they'd wind themselves around the parking meters. So I just held my breath and rode along, hoping nobody would be foolish enough to try grabbing at the harness. By the time we came to the intersection, they had let off a little of their steam and I gave them a good loud "Haw!" and they turned back out into the street. We were safely on our way out of town.

Those dogs really made me proud. We passed seventeen teams that first day and won the heat by more than ten minutes, running the whole twenty-five miles in just seconds over two hours. This time I didn't spend any time counting money in my head, not even after I eked out a win in the second heat. So far all I had was a couple of hundred dollars for the day prizes, not even enough to pay my expenses. The big pot, $2,500, went to the musher with the fastest total time, and I hadn't heard that anyone was throwing in the towel yet. Everything depended on that last day.

It dawned warm and rainy, the worst kind of weather for dog racing. When I got down to the starting chute I found out that trucks had been rolling into the city all night, dumping snow in the middle of Fourth Avenue so we could at least get the sleds out of town. I came down the chute slowly, but so had everyone else and I wasn't worried—until we got to the turn at Cordova Street. Standing right smack in the middle of the intersection was one of those photographers, his camera up to his eye, shooting away as though he were all alone somewhere taking pictures of a sunset. I could feel the dogs skitter off to the right, frightened and determined to get around that man by going straight up Fourth Avenue. Well, I don't know what he expected me to do—I had a lot riding on this race and I wasn't about to waste fifteen minutes getting my dogs back on course. I hollered "Gee!" and they turned, swinging in behind him and catching him just back of the knees with the towline. He went down and the camera went up—about twenty feet up—and I remember hoping he'd got good use out of it because when it came crashing down on that slush-covered pavement it splattered into no less than a dozen good-sized pieces.

That certainly whipped the dogs up. They pulled for all they were worth clear out to the flats where the going was a little smoother, and we passed our first team. At the twenty-mile checkpoint, they held up a sign saying that I was running second to the team just ahead. Pretty soon I could see him, crossing a small lake and holding the gap between us. Once we got off the ice, though, the trail was rough and I ran all the way, never setting a toe on the sled runner. And that's when my day-in, day-out training grind back home paid off: yard by yard I closed on him, passed him and was still going away, a full minute in the lead, when I crossed the finish line, winner of all three heats and the oldest man ever to win the All-Alaska Championship. I was dead beat, but still not so far gone that I didn't get down in the slush with those dogs and hug them until they whimpered.

I was mighty proud at the mushers' banquet that night.

Everybody said nice things about me, and they really pinned that "Huslia Hustler" title on me for good. They gave me the trophy, and there was a lot of clapping, and then they had me up on my feet to make a speech. If they'd told me to get out there on the floor and have a dance with a bear I couldn't have been less ready. But there they all were, quiet and waiting, and I took a deep breath and began to talk:

"Thank you very much. This cup is more important to me than the money." This was the strict truth because the money would hardly have a chance to get warm in my pocket: I owed almost every last cent of it, and the trophy was about all I'd be bringing home. "I'm going up to Fairbanks tomorrow and try to win me another one," I said. "I know a lot of you mushers will be going up there, too, and all I can say is I hope you don't make it as tough for me as you did down here."

There was a lot more clapping then and I figured I'd said enough, so I sat down. I was surprised at myself. I hadn't even let myself think about the North American Championship in Fairbanks until now. Oh, I suppose in the back of my mind I thought that if I did well in Anchorage, I'd give it a try. But I had trained myself and handled the dogs as though the All-Alaska race was the only one in the whole world. Now, without even thinking about it, I'd committed myself to the North American. I wasn't sorry. Anchorage had got me even. Fairbanks might yet get me that trading post.

I left early in the morning, driving easily and taking two full days to get there. This time I had some idea of what

I was doing and really enjoyed the trip. Besides, it was the first relaxation I'd had since the start of the year. When I got to town, the first thing I did was pay the dealer for the pickup and the people I owed for the losses on my freighting operation. That very afternoon I had the dogs out on the Chena, limbering them up and, from then on until the day of the race a week later, I was back on the same old training routine.

Every day more people poured into Fairbanks. Once more a field of over thirty mushers was entered in the race, including two of my old friends from Huslia, Bobby Vent and Bergman Sam. They'd been so stirred up by my win that they'd decided to have a try at big-time racing themselves. I wished them luck, but secretly hoped they'd go home. I knew those boys, and they could really go, and if there was one thing I didn't need it was more competition.

The winter carnival was in full swing, and anybody who wanted to could have gone from party to party twenty-four hours a day. Some of the mushers did, I guess, but I was carrying too many years for that kind of thing. I figured I had three hard days of racing left—two of twenty miles each, and the windup of thirty—and it seemed to be now or never for me. So I stuck to the dog trails and rope-skipping and gotten hours of sleep and kept telling myself that in a few days it would all be over.

It was warm the day of the first heat, and although the trail was good, built for speed, that sun was going to drain strength from the dogs. I got away well, running steadily, and by the halfway mark, just as though fate was working the whole thing, I could see that it was strictly between Bobby Vent and me. At each checkpoint the times separating us seemed to grow tighter, first Bobby ahead, then me. I gave it everything I owned coming in, and when they announced the results, I had won by one second.

I felt sorry for Bobby. He was no kid either, and we all knew that his big chance was to take that first heat while he was still fresh. Afterward he came to see me and said, "You're going all the way, Jimmy. I'll have to be satisfied with place money."

He didn't look like much of a fortuneteller at the end of the second day. Everything seemed all right going into the stretch. I was well ahead at the final checkpoint, and even eased up on the dogs, not pushing them at all so they'd have a lot left for the final race next day. We were actually in the chute—I could see the finish line!—when my leader dropped down right in his traces, lamed so badly he couldn't even walk. By the time I got him out of the harness and packed him back to the sled, I'd lost my lead and finished more than two and a half minutes behind Eddie Gallahorn, a hard-running young Eskimo from Kotzebue. Now I was second in total time and only thirty seconds ahead of the third-place team.

But the worst calamity was losing my leader, a dog who had won four out of five heats of championship racing, on the day before the last and most important race of all. Now I had no choice except to use my weary old Monkey in the lead, there just was no time to train a new dog for the job. As soon as the word got out, the gamblers started offering odds against me: one reason they're so hard to beat is that they never let sympathy for an underdog interfere with their cold judgment.

The people seemed to be with me, though. I could hear them calling as I reached the holding area that final afternoon: "Come on, old man! You can do it, old Jimmy!"

It didn't look good. The weather had stayed warm all three days, but today the thermometer had gone really freakish, right up to the middle forties. That was tough on everyone, true, but especially on an old leader and an older musher. I felt every day of all my years that afternoon, my strength worn down and my body aching with the hundred and fifteen grueling miles I'd run in the past two weeks. Today's course was to be the longest yet, thirty miles, with the extra ten miles of trail looped around Ship Creek, the ruggedest country in the area. We were to start at three-minute intervals in order of our standing; the Eskimo, Eddie Gallahorn, ahead of me, and a strapping strong Indian from Minto, Clarence Charlie, after me.

The Eskimo made a beautiful start, all twelve of his dogs running hard out of the chute. Poor Monkey looked lost up there at the head of the team, so I took time to go up and squat by him. I said, "Just this one more time, old dog. Then they can put us both out to pasture."

Then the timekeeper called out, "One minute to go!" And the gun went off and we came running down the chute between the great crowds of people and through all that yelling, and I knew we were making a slow start, but I forced myself not to push, not yet. We had a long way to go and if we didn't save something for the end, the heat and those last ten miles would kill us. All I wanted was to stay close to the Eskimo and ahead of Clarence Charlie.

It wasn't easy. That Indian was strong as a bull and pushed hard all the way. Every time I looked back, there he was, not a minute behind me. And in all the first twenty miles, I never saw Gallahorn up ahead and I began to worry that maybe my strategy was all wrong.

It was a brutally hard race. The heat took a lot out of

dogs and men, and team after team dropped by the wayside, just unable to go on. Of thirty-two starters, sixteen were scratched before the finish and one was disqualified.

I felt it, too. As I came up to the twenty-mile checkpoint, Clarence Charlie began closing on me. Then I saw Gallahorn was more than two minutes ahead, which meant that I had nearly five minutes of total time to make up in those last ten miles. Now there was no sense holding anything back—I'd have a lifetime of tomorrows to rest and think about this race—and I began to yell and push the sled up the hills, and the dogs really moved out. I thought we were going then. I thought we'd run that Eskimo down in no time at all.

And then came disaster. Off in the deep snow, a pair of moose moved away from us toward the cover of the spruce trees, and those dogs tore out after them as though their tails were on fire. I hollered and hauled back on the towline, but they dragged me through the snow like a plow. Finally I got my hands on the snub hook and caught hold of a jack spruce and that brought them up smartly, yapping, floundering in the snow—and fifty yards off the trail.

I was sick with discouragement and weariness. As I wallowed up toward the front of the team to straighten them out, my mouth felt as though it was full of cotton, and every breath I took hurt. I saw the spotter plane circling overhead. I could just imagine those guys up there reporting back to the announcer in town: "Oh, oh, Jimmy Huntington's had a rough break. His team has run off the trail and it looks like. . ."

The Indian passed me, going like a shot.

My first instinct was to clout those dogs dizzy. I didn't because, for one thing, I didn't have the strength to spare, and for another they knew well enough they'd done wrong. They huddled low and gave me that scared-stiff expression. I took Monkey's harness and led them all back to the trail, now maybe seven or eight minutes behind the leader, and Bergman Sam coming up on me from fourth place. I hollered, "Now come on, run, damn it! We're going to finish this race if it kills all thirteen of us!"

They went. Old Monkey dug in and pounded down the trail for all he was worth, and I yelled encouragement from behind, shoving that sled right up on the tail-enders. I didn't really think I had a chance, but I guess I'd been hoping for so long that I had the habit. Anyway, I never quit trying, snatching a breather by riding downhill, but running all the rest of the time.

Then, still five miles from the finish, I closed very fast on the team ahead—and it wasn't the Indian! As I flashed by, I could see the sweaty white look of exhaustion on Eddie Gallahorn's face. For three days and sixty-five miles that Eskimo had given it his all, leading the pack with the fastest total time. And now he just had nothing left to give and was limping in, fighting only to hang on so he could win a piece of place money. Later I'd feel sorry for him, but in that instant I only had room to feel one thing: if I caught the Indian, I could still win it all!

The trail began winding now, with another hill always following the one before. I don't know where I dredged up the strength, but I kept shoving that sled so the dogs didn't have to pull a pound. I could just see myself, with the famous Huntington luck, having a dog drop on me so that I'd have to haul him all the rest of the way in. That would be the end of everything.

I saw the buildings of the town in the distance and,

beneath them, a blurry black line on the white flats, Clarence Charlie's team. I struggled to remember how many seconds I'd had on him at the start and couldn't. My brain was fixed on one thing: to be sure of winning, I had to pass that Indian up ahead.

I tried to yell but the voice didn't sound like mine, a croaky "Run, Monkey!" that Monkey couldn't possibly hear. I banged on the sled with the snubbing hook, then it slipped from my fingers and fell by the trail. None of it mattered. The dogs were going on heart alone, and there just wasn't anything anyone could do now to make them go faster.

I don't know what I was going on. It didn't even seem to be me running alongside that sled, but some kind of mechanical man, soaked in sweat and unable to pull enough air into his lungs, or ever to quit plunging ahead, one painful, leaden step after another—a mechanical man running on hope.

But the Indian came closer. The black line was twelve dogs and a sled now, and a man struggling, as I was, on the trail. My dogs were staggering, only Monkey's pulling keeping them in line and moving ahead. I could see the bottom of the Indian's boots kicking snow back. I could see him leaning against his sled, half-pushing, half-sup-porting his own dead weight.

I passed Clarence Charlie just as we entered the chute. I didn't look at him. The great masses of people were a crowded blur in my eyes and only a terrific roar and an occasional voice—"Run, old man! Run!"—registered on my brain. I kept shoving the sled. That's all I knew how to do.

Then someone grabbed me and turned me loose from it. I sank to my knees, my chest bursting with pain, and not enough air in all the sky to satisfy me. There were people all around, and I shoved at them until I could see that someone was holding the dogs, unhooking them and caring for them. Then I fell all the way down in the snow and let them drag me off. I was satisfied, for those dogs were all I cared about at that moment. We were one thing.

Then there was a big hush in the crowd and somebody propped me up on a snowbank so I could see the announcer: "May I have your attention!" he called out. "Ladies and gentlemen, winner of the final heat by twenty-eight seconds, North American champion—and only the third man to ever win Alaska's two major dogsled races—Jim Huntington, the Huslia Husler!"

Then there came a thunder of cheering and applause. I felt tears in my eyes—I had actually done it—and I tried to stand up and thank everyone. But I was still a while from standing without help, so I just waved my hand at them, hoping they'd understand.

CHAPTER SIX

Starting Over

OH, IT WAS ALL SO GOOD in those first months after I came back home—to be with my family again, and all my friends, and know that my dream had come true. I had won a lot of money—$2,300, it turned out—and I was going to have my trading post at last.

But I would never race again. I was too old and finally had to admit it. I would have to leave the racing to the younger men in our town. And they did mighty well, all those Huslia Hustlers who came after me, men like Bergman Sam and Cui Biffelt, and all the others. Of course I didn't know it as I sat on the snowbank that March afternoon and felt the pain in my lungs ease, but they were to win half the major races of the next ten years, and Huslia would come to be known as the Dogsled Capital of the world. I'll always be proud that I had a part in starting that.

I fixed up the store just the way I wanted it, and when the ice went out my supplies came up on the riverboats, and the people would come around to buy and stay to talk about the old days or the big dogsled races. No man could have been happier with the shape of his dream when it finally turned real.

Then the next summer my wife left me, and in the early autumn the store burned down, and the house, and everything I owned in the world.

The fire started on a gray and blustering afternoon. Friday, September 27, 1957, was the kind of day that suddenly ends the Alaskan summer, the wind blowing a clear warning of freeze-up on the way. All morning I'd worked outside, sawing shelves for the store. Wayne, my youngest boy, was watching me. The other kids were in school.

A couple of times I looked up, and Wayne's big brown eyes were staring straight back at me. I wanted to tell him to quit sucking his thumb, but I didn't have the heart. He missed his mother. We all did. But Wayne was only three, and what could I say to console him? That she was coming back? She wasn't. That after twelve years of marriage and seven kids she just decided one fine summer day that she'd had it, and packed up and left us? That was the truth, and that's all there was to say.

After a while the boy said he was cold, and I sent him into the house. "Don't touch anything in the store," I said. "Stay in the back." I went on with my sawing, head down, never noticing the dirty gray smoke seeping out from under the roof logs. The first I knew of the trouble was when someone yelled at me from down by the riverbank:

"Jimmy! Jim Huntington! Your house is on fire!"

I looked up and saw the smoke. I stood rooted there while people scrambled up the bank toward me. Then I ran for the house calling, "Wayne! Wayne!"

I threw the door open and was hit by a rush of hot smoke. Inside, orange flame shot back and forth, grabbing for the rows of canned goods, the bolts of cloth that only came in last week—everything.

"Wayne!" I yelled again. I backed off a step and ran in low, still hollering, trying to see something through the fire and the gray smoke. I didn't know what to do. It was all going—the beaver pelts, magazines, ivory carvings—everything I had in the world, twenty-five years of bitter hard work, and I couldn't stop it. I began snatching up whatever I could reach, boxes of Baby Ruth and O Henry bars, but they spilled from my arms and I kept stepping on them. And all the time I was edging toward the back, calling my boy.

Choking, trying to find some air to breathe, I fell to my knees. I was close to our living quarters and they seemed to be a roaring mass of fire. My lungs hurt and my hands were seared from the heat of the floor—it smoked and buckled and would burst into flame any second—but I crept on. In my head I had this picture of poor little Wayne, caught in there and scared to death, crying for me to help him.

I must have passed out. I had a blurry feeling that someone was dragging me toward the door, and they couldn't have done that, no one could have pulled me out of there if I had all my senses. Outside, I sucked in fresh air like a man who'd been drowning. But just as soon as my head cleared, I broke away from whoever was holding me and tore for the house. Running, I grabbed a gunny sack up from the ground and was trying to pull it over my head when they tackled me and said I couldn't go back in there, and held me down while I fought them and called for Wayne. Then there came that explosion and all the windows blew out and the roof caved in with a fiery crash of sparks and smoke, and finally I lay still. It was too late now, all too late. A woman crossed herself, and I said, "My poor little kid."

They walked me away. I saw people running up from the river with buckets of water. But all they could hope to do was wet down the next house and the outbuildings, for the wind was blowing whip-hard and you could just see those flames reaching out for something else to latch onto. One of the men came over and said, "Looks like the wind blew through an open window on the north side and tipped over the kerosene lamp. That's how she started."

Somebody brought my kids from the schoolhouse. They walked real slow, their faces white and scared, and I tried to put my arms around all of them and hold them near to me. They began to cry, even the older ones, for they had never seen their father so busted up.

And then, all of a sudden, Wayne was there. One of the men came pounding up the hill—and he was hauling Wayne by the hand! Wayne, safe and well—alive!

"He was down playing with the dogs. Jimmy, he never even went in the house. He didn't know what was happening up here! I just now saw him and..."

I suppose I began to cry then. I was so mixed up. I grabbed that little kid and squeezed him against me so hard his bones must have ached. "Where'd you go?" I mumbled. "I thought you were in there. I thought you were a goner..."

When I let him go he put his thumb in his mouth, and tears stood in his big eyes, and I tried to smile so he wouldn't be so frightened. Not that I had anything to smile about. A life's labor had gone up in smoke. Everything but the clothes on my back—the store, supplies I hadn't paid for, our home, even our food for the winter—was burned down to a smoldering heap of ashes. It was all gone.

I sat shivering on a stump under the darkening sky and stared at the ruins, tormented with remembering how long I had struggled to get this far in life. You might say I'd been twenty-five years getting that trading post built, and every last thing that went into it was bought with the sweat of my brow. My father had pounded it into me that this was one way for a hardworking man to make out in this country, to have the respect of his people, and a decent living when he was too old to live off the land.

The things I'd done to make a dollar! I'd hunted wolves for the bounty. I'd run a trap line and hauled freight and piloted a riverboat on the Yukon. When other men my age were riding in their sleds, I was still running full speed behind mine, training my dogs all winter so that maybe I could pick up a little extra cash in the mushing races at Anchorage and Fairbanks. And I'd plowed it all into that store, into my hopes of making something of myself. But it wasn't until this summer, past my fortieth birthday, that I could afford to move us all into the back of the cabin and open for business up front.

My goal was always the same, to have that store, and to use it to prove to my people, once and for all, that we were as good as any white man. All anyone had to do was work and want it badly enough and he had to make good. "Look at me," I'd tell them. "Nobody's ever going to wag his head over me and say, 'Poor Jimmy.'"

And now that's exactly what they were doing. The whole village was there, and they were all looking at me, and there was pity in every eye.

I felt old and very tired. I didn't see how I could possibly start all over again. It had taken me all my grown-up years just to get back to where my father had been, and in a few minutes I'd lost it all.

Suddenly, I understood how easy it could be for a Native to give up and drift down to the white man's towns, living off the occasional laborer's job he might get, or whatever he could beg, and all the time trying to lose himself and his fears in whiskey. Was that what was in the cards for me after all the years of trying? Would my kids be better off if I just quit and went off somewhere and left it up to the village or the Territory to look after them?

For weeks I just hung around, thinking about all the things that had happened to me and wondering what to do next. One day I'd decide to go out on the trap line, and the next that I'd better set to work and rebuild my cabin, and the one after that I'd fly down to Fairbanks or Anchorage and look for wages. But all of it seemed pointless and painful, like banging your head against a stone wall. I'd tried—Lord, how I'd tried—and what had it all come to? Where would I find the strength to hope that anything could be different if I tried one more time? And so I did nothing, just moved my family in with some friends and sat brooding on the riverbank all the hours of the day.

Then, in the middle of October, a bush pilot landed at our town, and on the spur of the moment I made up my mind what I was going to do. I asked him if he would fly me up to a place on the Dakili River where I knew the marten trapping was good, and that very afternoon I was setting up a camp there. Maybe it wasn't the smartest thing to do, but at least it was something. My kids would be looked after, and I hoped that a couple of months alone in the bush would help me sort out the odds and ends of my life. Maybe by Christmas, when the pilot was supposed to come back for me, I'd know what to do with the rest of my life.

One thing, the old routine of making a camp in the woods, of preparing to live off the land and defend yourself against it, soothed away some of the hurts of civilization. There wasn't time to think about them. They weren't the most important things in the world anymore, not as important as cutting wood so you wouldn't freeze to death, or pitching a good snug tent so you wouldn't be buried by an overnight snowfall. I worked hard and tried not to think about anything but the thing I was doing.

I spent a week setting out the traps, and then ran them every day. It was a lot different without the dogs. To cover the ground, I had to start before dawn and it was well after dark when I got in. I used a candle inside a tin can for a traveling light, and there was not a creature to say a word to, not a dog to scold or praise, not an animal stirring in the bitter cold of that winter.

In December it turned the coldest ever. I hadn't brought a thermometer so I never knew what the temperature was, but I knew that no bush plane could fly in that kind of weather. Even with a fire going, the tent was freezing cold, and I slept in parka, mittens, and mukluks. On the twenty-first, when the pilot was supposed to come, the worst of the cold seemed over and I sat in the tent listening for that airplane engine all day. I had thirty marten skins and a few minks, a good catch, and I thought that at least I could make a nice Christmas for the kids.

But the pilot didn't come that day, or the day after. I couldn't leave the camp for fear that he'd land while I was gone. I just sat there, hour after endless hour, straining to hear some sound in the deathly wilderness quiet, thinking the old crippling thoughts—and some new ones: now I wouldn't even be with my kids for Christmas—a sure sign that I hadn't yet come up with the answers about my future.

On the fourth day it was colder than ever and I knew no airplane was coming after me. I cached the skins, fixed a light pack, and set out on foot. It was eighty miles to Huslia.

In the beginning I walked hard just to keep warm. I made only two stops a day for tea and kept walking well after dark because there was very little daylight. The first night it was so cold I didn't sleep at all, just rested for six hours and then put on my pack and snowshoes and started out again. The second night, when I did sleep, it snowed, and if some deep-down instinct hadn't wakened me early, I'd have been smothered under the silent, seven-foot fall. Once more I moved on, suffering now from the cold and a growing weakness, yet heartened, somehow, by the battle. This I understood. This was a man against the wilderness, and if the odds were against me, at least I knew what they were. And fighting something I could feel and see, I pushed on, and felt stronger.

Late on the night of the fourth day, I was little more than five miles from the town. I was very tired now, hardly moving. But I had reached the big flats, and there was nothing to make a fire with so I had to keep going. I wanted to drop my pack and leave it but all my years in the bush told me I couldn't: if I was forced to stop, my blanket would be my last chance at survival.

Three hours later I had come to the patch of willows just outside the town. I knew I'd make it now—if I hollered loud enough they'd hear and come get me—but I wasn't about to stagger in there near-frozen and half-dead. I broke off some dry branches and made a fire. I melted snow for a tea. And as my strength came back I thought about my mother and the end of her long journey. I wondered if I had her courage, if I could have gone on another nine hundred miles—if I could still do anything useful with my life.

It was past two in the morning when I knocked on my friends' door, waking them out of a sound sleep so that they looked at me as though I were a ghost. The husband read the thermometer outside the window: it was sixty-four degrees below zero. Not once in the past month, he told me, had it ever crept above fifty below. His wife cooked me a hot meal, and we talked in whispers so we wouldn't wake my kids. I wanted to see them, but even more I wanted to close my eyes and go to sleep in that nice warm house and sleep for a long, long time.

It didn't seem that I'd slept at all when I heard Wayne's voice crying out, "Daddy's back! Daddy's back!" Then they were all yelling and clambering over the bed, jabbing me with their knees and elbows as they squirmed to get the spot next to Daddy. And I thought, well, I can sleep tomorrow. Right now it was sweeter to hold them near me and look at their faces and listen to their nonsense.

And suddenly, as I did, it was as though a part of my mind cleared of the fog that had hold of it and I could look out on all my tomorrows. I saw myself going to work to rebuild the cabin and, in summer, using my marten-catch money to take the kids down to Anchorage where I'd get a job. I was well known in Anchorage now; surely there would be work for me. Maybe I'd freight a little, or even pilot the bigger boats—nobody knew these rivers the way I did. In the winter I could trap again, slowly building my stake until I could put that store together one more time. Maybe I'd even marry again. These kids deserved a mother, and I deserved a friend.

I sat up straight in the bed, looking dead ahead of me into that future that once more seemed possible. The kids fell quiet and I pulled them close. Then I said, "Let's get up and going, you guys! We've got work to do!"

That's about the way it turned out—the job, the piloting, the new store, all of it, and, in 1962, a fine wife. I still get scared when I think how easily I could have given it all up back there in those dark days after the fire. And so I treasure this good new life, and I tell my people that it can be done, almost anything can be done. No one ever promised me, or promised any man—Indian, Eskimo, or white man—that life was easy in this country. You had to fight for whatever was important to you. You had to be tough. Maybe it's a little harder for a half-breed. Maybe it takes a little longer. But it can be done.

AFTERWORD

NEXT TO THE LAST TIME I saw Jimmy Huntington, he was a patient at the Alaska Native Medical Center in Anchorage and I thought he was dying. He looked terrible, slumped down into his pillow, shrunken. "What's the matter with you?" I asked, trying to be ready for the worst.

"They say I got a cancer in my nose."

Not ready for that, I fumbled my way into a chair, looking away. Then I looked back and said, "What are they doing about it?"

"So far, nothing. When I ask why they don't just take it out, they roll their eyes and give me doctor double-talk. They say, 'Ah, it's not as simple as that.'" He raised his head from the pillow and snorted, "That's bull"—using both syllables.

He was not a happy man. Jimmy was, above all, plainspoken. Beating around the bush was not his style;

weasel words unnerved him. Cancer was one thing, one of life's dirty tricks, okay; but being patronized was not to be borne. And he must have been miserable in that hospital, penned up in the middle of the biggest city in Alaska when he could at most tolerate a bush village and was only truly at peace under the big sky.

It was the spring of 1967. I had known Jimmy only a couple of years but we had written a book together, the story of his life, and there were no secrets between us. I never asked a question he didn't answer with the straight truth that was his trademark. And he asked plenty of his own questions, poking around in my past until he knew almost as much about me as I did about him. And when you have gone through all that with someone and still friends, you're good friends.

"Is there anything I can do for you, Jim?" I asked, thinking maybe he wanted to send a message to his children, some final thoughts.

"I wouldn't mind some candy," he said.

"Candy," I repeated dumbly. Was that what he'd said? Candy?

"Yeah. You know nobody comes to this place for the food."

I offered to go get it right away but he said, no, tomorrow would do. It would give him something to look forward to. I only hoped they wouldn't have moved him out to the morgue by the time I came back with it. But no, when I showed up the next day he was sitting up in bed and looking more like himself, maybe not yet ready to get dressed and go out to check his trap lines, but better. "Hey, waiting for candy sure seems to pep you up," I said.

"I hope you brought enough," he answered.

It was typical. I could tell that he had thought the thing through and as there was nothing he could do about the cancer, he turned his attention elsewhere: What was I working on? How were the sales of our book doing? He told me he was going to give "those guys" another week and then he was going home.

And, remarkably, that's just what he did. I never found out what happened to his cancer; he never even mentioned it again. But with or without it, Jimmy went on to live his life, another auspicious and productive 20 years of it.

My work took me a world away from Alaska, and though we stayed in touch and I always kept track of him and his life in politics, I never saw him again. But if I sit down with a drink and open one of his letters, there he sits, spinning stories like the ones in this book— deploring politicians, extolling Alaska, planning a moose hunt down the Yukon in his flat-bottomed boat.

He stayed what he was, a hunter and a trapper. And having grown up and lived all his life in Huslia or one or another of the Native villages along the Yukon and Koyukuk river basins, his concerns were those of the people scattered over that immensity of interior Alaska, a sweep of land bigger than any state, and more sparsely settled.

But it didn't end there. Jimmy had been gifted with rare common sense and the ability to make clear the issues that mattered to his people—subsistence, schools, land claims, fish and game laws. People listened when he spoke. And as his name was recognized and respected nearly everywhere in the state—not only as an Alaska sled-dog racing champion, the original Huslia Hustler, but as a wilderness man who cared about the wilderness—there was hardly a time through the '60s and '70s when he wasn't serving on some fish or game regulatory board.

In November 1974, he ran for election to the Alaska state legislature as a write-in candidate and won—but didn't find out about it until well into December because he was off in the bush running his trap lines. Then, before the legislature convened, when he was back out trapping in temperatures that dropped past 50 below zero, he was hit by a massive heart attack. Somehow he made it back to Huslia on his own and was flown to Anchorage for open heart surgery. He had to take his oath of office over a hospital telephone.

But if Jimmy got off to a late start in the House of Representatives, he caught up fast—to the considerable discomfort of a good many of his fellow lawmakers. He was one of only a bare handful of Native Alaskans in the legislature, and none spoke out more eloquently about problems of the Native people, nor more bluntly on their behalf against vested interests in the Lower 48 and in Anchorage and Fairbanks. He once famously told legislative colleagues that there were among them people making laws for the North country who knew nothing about it. "Some of you people from Anchorage," he said, "when you turn north on Lake Otis Parkway, you think you're in the wilderness."

Veteran Alaska newsman Bill Tobin tells of Jimmy's letter to the *Anchorage Times* about the notorious 1976 legislative session in Juneau that had stretched out for more than 100 days, at the taxpayers' expense. "We are not only dragging our feet down here," he wrote, "we are dragging our ass." A few days later, according to Tobin, he stood up and told the dumbstruck House that their long-winded orations were "uncalled for and damned foolishness... you're all just squirming around, thinking of how you can fool the public." No one rose to argue the point.

He never gave up fighting for the people of Alaska, not even when heart trouble slowed him down and then laid him low. "I'll be back," he told his kids that night of February 21, 1987, when the medical evacuation plane came to fly him out to the hospital in Fairbanks. But it was not to be. He died in mid-flight, leaving seven children, eight grandchildren and a uniquely Alaskan legacy. He was 72.

"His life was a full one," said the *Times* in an editorial. "He served well. Alaska is richer because he was here."

I am only sorry he is not here to see this splendid new edition of his life story.

Lawrence Elliott, who has written several books and numerous magazine articles, was Reader's Digest correspondent for Alaska and western Canada when this book was written in the mid-1960s. Elliott now lives in Luxembourg.

www.ingramcontent.com/pod-product-compliance
Lightning Source LLC
Chambersburg PA
CBHW070721240426
43673CB00003B/95